Sourdough

Revolution

Empower Your Kitchen with the Ultimate Guide to Satisfying Bread and Tantalizing Recipes| Full Colour Edition

Gloria J. Williams

Editor: AALIYAH LYONS

Interior Design: BROOKE WHITE

Cover Art: DANIELLE REES

Food stylist: Sienna Adams

Table Of Contents

Introduction

In the ever-evolving world of culinary delights, where trends come and go, one thing remains constant: the timeless art of baking. From the dawn of civilization to the modern-day kitchen, bread has been a staple, a symbol of nourishment, and a source of comfort. and in the United Kingdom, one particular bread has been quietly rising to the forefront of our culinary consciousness: sourdough.

Within these pages, you will discover not just a collection of recipes but a profound appreciation for the craft of sourdough bread-making, a craft that has captivated the hearts and taste buds of many.

Sourdough is more than just a type of bread; it is a living tradition that bridges the past and the present. The origins of sourdough can be traced back thousands of years, and it has journeyed through time, adapting to the diverse landscapes of the United Kingdom. Each region and each baker has added its unique twist, resulting in a rich tapestry of flavors and techniques that you will explore in this cookbook.

What sets sourdough apart is its simplicity, yet paradoxically, its complexity. It is made from the humblest of ingredients: flour, water, and salt. However, it is the wild yeast and lactic acid bacteria that dance in harmony, creating that distinctive tang and chewy texture, which elevates sourdough to an artisanal level of baking.

But sourdough is more than just the sum of its ingredients. It is a testament to patience, to the slow and deliberate process of fermentation. It teaches us to savor the moment, to appreciate the journey as much as the destination. As you embark on your sourdough adventure, you will come to understand that time is not an enemy but a trusted ally, and patience is a virtue that rewards the diligent baker with a perfect loaf.

In this cookbook, you will find a treasure trove of recipes that range from the classic to the inventive, from the traditional to the avant-garde. Whether you are a seasoned baker looking to hone your sourdough skills or a novice embarking on your first loaf, there is something here for everyone. The recipes have been carefully crafted and meticulously tested, ensuring that your journey through these pages will be a rewarding and delicious one.

But this cookbook is more than just a collection of recipes. It is a celebration of community, of the shared passion for sourdough that unites bakers and bread lovers across the United Kingdom. As you dive into these recipes, you are joining a fraternity of bakers who have embraced the art of sourdough, each with their unique story and perspective.

This cookbook is a tribute to the artisans, the home bakers, the pioneers who have kept the flame of sourdough burning bright across the UK. It is a testament to the power of bread to bring people together, to nourish not just our bodies but also our souls.

As you embark on your sourdough journey, remember that the beauty of sourdough lies not just in the final loaf but in the process, the experimentation, the community, and the sheer joy of creating something wonderful with your own hands. So, roll up your sleeves, dust your hands with flour, and let the magic of sourdough take you on a culinary adventure that spans generations and transcends time.

Chapter 1

The Art of Sourdough

Rich History of Sourdough

In the world of culinary delights, there are few things as enduring and universally cherished as bread. From the earliest days of human civilization to the modern era, bread has remained a staple of our diets, an essential part of our cultures, and a symbol of nourishment and sustenance. and among the diverse array of bread varieties, one stands out for its rich history, complex flavors, and deep cultural significance: sourdough.

ANCIENT ORIGINS

The history of sourdough can be traced back thousands of years, making it one of the oldest known forms of leavened bread. Its story begins in the cradle of civilization, where ancient Egyptians and Mesopotamians first discovered the magical process of fermentation. Wild yeasts, present in the environment, would naturally interact with flour and water mixtures left out in the open air, causing them to bubble and rise. The result was a tangy, chewy bread that we now know as sourdough.

THE RISE OF SOURDOUGH IN EUROPE

Sourdough's journey through history is closely intertwined with the development of European baking traditions. As the Roman Empire expanded, so did the popularity of sourdough bread. Roman soldiers carried sourdough starter cultures with them as they conquered new lands, spreading the art of sourdough baking throughout Europe. This cultural exchange eventually led to the creation of various regional sourdough breads, each with its unique characteristics.

SOURDOUGH IN THE UNITED KINGDOM

The United Kingdom has its own rich history with sourdough. Traditional British bread-making methods have always leaned toward yeastless bread, and sourdough fit the bill perfectly. Throughout history, different regions of the UK have developed their own sourdough variations, reflecting the local ingredients and baking techniques. From the hearty Scottish oatcakes to the distinctive Irish soda bread, sourdough has left its flavorful mark on the British Isles.

THE GOLD RUSH AND SOURDOUGH IN AMERICA

Sourdough also played a pivotal role in the history of the United States, particularly during the Gold Rush era in California. Miners and pioneers carried sourdough starter cultures with them on their arduous journeys, relying on this reliable source of sustenance. The famous "sourdoughs" of the Gold Rush era were not just bread but a symbol of resilience and resourcefulness. To this day, San Francisco sourdough is renowned for its unique flavor, thanks to the city's distinctive wild yeast strains.

THE SCIENCE OF SOURDOUGH

Beyond its historical significance, sourdough is a fascinating subject in the world of microbiology and food science. At the heart of sourdough bread-making are wild yeast and lactic acid bacteria. These microscopic organisms form symbiotic relationships within the sourdough starter, converting sugars in the flour into carbon dioxide gas and lactic acid. This dual fermentation process creates the characteristic rise, texture, and tangy flavor of sourdough.

- Health Benefits in Sourdough

Sourdough bread, with its delightful tangy flavor and chewy texture, has been a staple in the diets of many cultures for centuries. Beyond its delicious taste and versatile uses, sourdough offers a range of health benefits that make it a wise choice for those seeking both nourishment and flavor in their daily bread. In this exploration of the health benefits of sourdough, we will uncover the nutritional advantages, digestive benefits, and potential impact on overall well-being that this ancient bread brings to our modern tables.

NUTRITIONAL RICHES OF SOURDOUGH

One of the key health benefits of sourdough lies in its impressive nutritional profile. This fermented bread is a treasure trove of essential nutrients that contribute to a balanced diet. Here are some of the notable nutritional components found in sourdough:Improved Digestibility: Sourdough's unique fermentation process breaks down complex starches and proteins, making it easier to digest. This transformation can be particularly beneficial for individuals with gluten sensitivities or mild gluten intolerance.

- Lower Glycemic Index: Sourdough has a lower glycemic index compared to many other types of bread. This means it has a slower and more gradual impact on blood sugar levels, which can be advantageous for individuals seeking better blood sugar control.
- Beneficial Bacteria: the fermentation of sourdough encourages the growth of beneficial bacteria, such as lactobacilli. These probiotic microorganisms may contribute to improved gut health and enhanced immune function.
- Rich in Vitamins and Minerals: Sourdough bread contains essential vitamins and minerals, including B vitamins (such as folate, riboflavin, and niacin), iron, magnesium, and selenium. These nutrients play crucial roles in various bodily functions, from energy metabolism to immune support.
- Prebiotic Potential: Sourdough also contains prebiotics, which are indigestible fibers that serve as food for beneficial gut bacteria. This can further promote a healthy gut microbiome.

DIGESTIVE BENEFITS OF SOURDOUGH

The fermentation process that gives sourdough its distinctive flavor also contributes to its digestive advantages. Here's how sourdough can benefit your digestive system:

- Gluten Digestibility: While sourdough is not gluten-free, the fermentation process reduces the levels of gluten, making it more digestible for some individuals with gluten sensitivities. However, those with celiac disease should still exercise caution and choose certified gluten-free products.
- Phytic Acid Reduction: Sourdough fermentation reduces the phytic acid content in the bread. Phytic acid can interfere with the absorption of minerals like iron, zinc, and calcium. By lowering phytic acid levels, sourdough enhances the bioavailability of these essential minerals.
- Enhanced Nutrient Absorption: the beneficial bacteria in sourdough can improve nutrient absorption in the gut. This means that the vitamins and minerals present in sourdough and other foods you consume with it may be absorbed more efficiently by your body.
- Improved Gut Microbiome: Sourdough's prebiotic potential can support the growth of beneficial bacteria in your gut, promoting a balanced and diverse gut microbiome. A healthy gut microbiome is linked to numerous health benefits, including a strong immune system and better digestion.
- Reduced Digestive Discomfort: For some individuals, sourdough is easier on the digestive system, resulting in reduced bloating, gas, and discomfort compared to conventionally leavened bread.

BEYOND NUTRITION: THE SOULFUL CONNECTION

While the nutritional and digestive benefits of sourdough are substantial, there is another dimension to its appeal that extends beyond the physical benefits. Sourdough embodies a sense of tradition, culture, and craftsmanship that nourishes the soul as well. Here's how sourdough fosters this unique connection:

- Heritage and Tradition: Sourdough is steeped in tradition and history, carrying the flavors and stories of generations past. Baking sourdough is a way to connect with the culinary heritage of diverse cultures, from San Francisco to the Mediterranean.
- The Art of Patience: Sourdough teaches us the value of patience and mindfulness in the kitchen. The process of nurturing a sourdough starter, waiting for the dough to rise, and baking it to perfection encourages a sense of presence and appreciation for the journey.
- Community and Sharing: Sourdough has a way of bringing people together. The act of sharing a freshly baked loaf with friends or family fosters a sense of community and connection, nourishing not just our bodies but our social bonds as well.
- A Creative Canvas: Sourdough is a versatile medium for culinary creativity. Bakers can experiment with different flours, seeds, herbs, and spices to create unique and personalized loaves, making each batch a work of art.
- Mindful Eating: the distinct flavor and texture of sourdough encourage mindful eating. Savoring each bite of this bread allows us to fully appreciate its complexity and the craftsmanship that went into its creation.

Cultural Significance Found in Sourdough

In the world of culinary traditions, few foods hold as much cultural significance and historical resonance as sourdough bread. Beyond its delightful tangy flavor and chewy texture, sourdough carries with it a rich tapestry of cultural heritage that has been woven through centuries and across continents. In this exploration of the cultural significance found in sourdough, we will uncover the deep-rooted connections, stories, and rituals that make this bread a cherished symbol of tradition and unity.

A SHARED HERITAGE ACROSS BORDERS

Sourdough's cultural significance extends across borders and transcends language barriers. Whether you're in San Francisco enjoying a classic sourdough loaf or in the heart of France savoring a pain au levain, the presence of sourdough connects you to a shared heritage that spans the globe.

- The Mediterranean Legacy: Sourdough has deep roots in the Mediterranean, where ancient civilizations like the Egyptians and Greeks embraced the art of fermentation. In these regions, sourdough was not just a staple; it was a symbol of life itself. The act of nurturing a sourdough starter, with its mixture of flour and water, paralleled the cycle of life and growth in nature. It represented the continuation of traditions through generations.
- Sourdough on the American Frontier: the cultural significance of sourdough reached new heights during the American frontier era. Pioneers, prospectors, and settlers carried sourdough starters with them on their treacherous journeys westward. The resilient "sourdoughs" of the Wild West became not only bakers but also symbols of survival and tenacity.
- Breaking Bread Together: Sourdough is often associated with communal gatherings and celebrations. Breaking bread, particularly sourdough bread, has been a cherished ritual in various cultures around the world. It symbolizes unity, hospitality, and the act of coming together to share a meal. In many cultures, sourdough bread is considered a token of friendship and a symbol of welcoming guests.
- Sourdough's Place in Religious Traditions: Sourdough's cultural significance is not limited to secular contexts. It holds a place in religious traditions as well. In Eastern Orthodox Christianity, for example, sourdough bread plays a central role in the preparation of prosphora, the bread used in the Eucharist. The act of baking and offering sourdough

prosphora is a sacred ritual that connects the faithful to their spiritual heritage.

- Cultural Adaptations: Sourdough has a remarkable ability to adapt to different cultures and environments. As it traveled the world, it absorbed the flavors and ingredients of each region it encountered. This adaptability is evident in the diverse sourdough variations found across the United Kingdom, Europe, and beyond. From Scottish oatcakes to Italian ciabatta, each sourdough bread tells a story of cultural exchange and adaptation.

CRAFTSMANSHIP AND TRADITION

Sourdough bread is not just a product; it is a labor of love and a testament to craftsmanship. The act of making sourdough involves a deep understanding of the dough's behavior, the fermentation process, and the subtleties of flavor development. This artisanal approach to bread-making is a celebration of tradition and heritage.

- Passing Down Knowledge: Sourdough is often passed down from one generation to the next. Many families have treasured sourdough starters that have been nurtured and maintained for decades, if not centuries. This passing down of knowledge and the sharing of starter cultures are a way of preserving cultural heritage and ensuring that traditions endure.
- Regional Identity: Sourdough is deeply intertwined with regional identities. Each sourdough variation reflects the local ingredients, climate, and baking techniques of its place of origin. of Scandinavia or the airy baguette of France, these breads are emblematic of the unique culinary heritage of their regions.
- Celebratory Baking: In many cultures, sourdough bread is reserved for special occasions and celebrations. Weddings, holidays, and festivals often feature specially crafted sourdough loaves that carry symbolic significance. These breads become an integral part of the cultural fabric, adding depth and meaning to the festivities.
- Cultural Exchange Through Food: Food has always been a vehicle for cultural exchange, and sourdough is no exception. The sharing of sourdough recipes and techniques has fostered connections between people of different backgrounds, fostering a sense of unity and shared experiences.

Unique Flavor Development within Sourdough

Sourdough bread, with its distinctively tangy flavor and complex aroma, has captured the palates and hearts of bread enthusiasts around the world. Beyond its delightful texture and versatility, sourdough's greatest allure lies in its remarkable ability to undergo a nuanced and fascinating flavor transformation during the fermentation process. In this exploration of the unique flavor development within sourdough, we will uncover the science and art behind its taste, the influence of variables, and how sourdough becomes a canvas for culinary creativity.

THE FOUNDATIONS OF FLAVOR

At its core, sourdough's unique flavor development is a result of microbial fermentation. This complex transformation begins when wild yeast and lactic acid bacteria, present in the environment or added as a starter culture, interact with the flour and water mixture. This interaction sets in motion a series of chemical reactions that give rise to sourdough's distinctive taste profile:

- Acidity: One of the primary contributors to sourdough's flavor is its acidity. During fermentation, lactic acid and acetic acid are produced by the bacteria. These acids not only lend a pleasing tartness but also act as natural preservatives, enhancing the bread's shelf life.
- Carbon Dioxide Gas: As yeast consumes sugars in the dough, it releases carbon dioxide gas. This gas is trapped within the dough's gluten matrix, causing it to rise. The formation of bubbles and the resulting open crumb structure contribute to the overall texture and mouthfeel.
- Aromatic Compounds: Sourdough fermentation produces a wide range of aromatic compounds, including esters, aldehydes, and ketones. These compounds are responsible for the diverse and complex aromas that emanate from freshly baked sourdough bread.
- Nutty and Caramel Notes: Maillard reactions, which occur between amino acids and reducing sugars during baking, contribute to the development of nutty and caramel-like flavors in the crust and crumb. These reactions are more pronounced in sourdough due to its extended fermentation period.

VARIABLES INFLUENCING FLAVOR

Sourdough's flavor development is not a one-size-fits-all process. It can vary significantly based on a multitude of factors, allowing bakers to craft a wide range of flavor profiles. Some of the key variables that influence sourdough's taste include:

- Fermentation Time: the duration of fermentation profoundly affects the flavor. Longer fermentation periods allow for more pronounced acidity and a deeper, complex taste. Shorter fermentations result in milder flavors.
- Temperature: Temperature plays a crucial role in shaping sourdough's flavor. Warmer temperatures encourage faster fermentation and can lead to a more pronounced tangy taste, while cooler temperatures result in a milder, subtler flavor.
- Flour Type: the type of flour used, whether it's all-purpose, whole wheat, rye, or a blend, imparts its unique flavor to the sourdough. Whole-grain flours tend to produce earthier, nuttier notes, while white flours result in a lighter taste.Hydration Level: the hydration level of the dough, or the ratio of water to flour, affects the dough's texture and ultimately its flavor. Higher hydration doughs tend to produce a more open crumb structure and a complex flavor profile.
- Starter Culture: the specific strains of yeast and lactic acid bacteria in the starter culture influence the flavor development. A well-maintained, mature starter can contribute to a more consistent and pronounced sourdough taste.

CULINARY CREATIVITY WITH SOURDOUGH

Sourdough is not just about the science of fermentation; it's also a canvas for culinary creativity. Bakers and chefs around the world experiment with a variety of ingredients and techniques to create unique sourdough flavor experiences:
- Infusions: Herbs, spices, seeds, and dried fruits can be added to the dough to infuse it with distinctive flavors. Rosemary and olive sourdough, for example, combines the earthy aroma of rosemary with the brininess of olives.

- Multigrain Blends: Combining different types of flours and grains, such as spelt, barley, or oats, can result in multi-layered flavors and added nutritional depth.
- Long Fermentation: Extended fermentation periods, sometimes spanning several days, can intensify the sourdough's taste. This method, known as "retardation," is a hallmark of traditional artisanal bread-making.
- Specialty Starters: Some bakers use unique starters, such as fruit-based starters or those derived from specific geographical regions, to impart distinct regional or fruity notes to their sourdough.
- Tasting Notes: Like wine connoisseurs, some bread enthusiasts explore sourdough with a discerning palate, noting flavor nuances such as fruity, nutty, tangy, or floral qualities.

SOURDOUGH AROUND THE WORLD

the beauty of sourdough lies in its adaptability to various cultural contexts. Around the world, sourdough bread is celebrated in diverse ways, reflecting local tastes and traditions. Here are a few examples:

- San Francisco Sourdough: Known for its particularly pronounced tangy flavor, San Francisco sourdough owes its distinct taste to the city's unique wild yeast strains. This sourdough has become a symbol of the city itself.
- French Pain au Levain: French sourdough, or "pain au levain," is celebrated for its rustic and slightly sour taste. It is an essential component of French cuisine, used for everything from baguettes to boules.
- Eastern European Rye Sourdough: In Eastern Europe, rye sourdough is a staple. Its robust, earthy flavor complements hearty traditional dishes like pierogi and sauerkraut.
- Indian Naan: Even in regions where flatbreads are more common, sourdough finds its place. Indian naan bread, with its mild tang, is a perfect accompaniment to curries and stews.
- Mexican Boli: In Mexico, bolillos, a type of sourdough roll, are cherished for their slightly sour taste and crisp crust. They are used for making tortas, sandwiches filled with various ingredients.

Chapter 2

Getting Started with Sourdough

In the world of bread-making, there's nothing quite as magical as a sourdough starter. This humble mixture of flour and water, left to ferment, captures wild yeast and friendly bacteria from its environment, giving rise to a living, breathing ecosystem. A sourdough starter is more than just a leavening agent; it's the heartbeat of sourdough baking, responsible for the distinct flavor, texture, and character that set sourdough bread apart from all others. In this exploration of the sourdough starter, we'll delve into what it is, how it works, and why it holds such a revered place in the world of culinary traditions.

What is a Sourdough Starter?

At its essence, a sourdough starter is a mixture of flour and water in which naturally occurring wild yeast and lactic acid bacteria, primarily lactobacilli, form a symbiotic relationship. This harmonious microbial community thrives on the carbohydrates in the flour and water, converting them into carbon dioxide gas and various organic acids, most notably lactic and acetic acids.

the result of this fermentation process is a living, bubbly, and tangy mixture that is the soul of sourdough baking. The starter acts as both the leavening agent and the flavor developer for sourdough bread, imbuing it with its characteristic sour taste, complex aroma, and chewy texture.

HOW DOES A SOURDOUGH STARTER WORK?

the magic of a sourdough starter lies in the way it harnesses the power of wild microorganisms to ferment the dough. Here's how it works:

- Capture and Inoculation: When you create a sourdough starter, you mix flour and water and expose the mixture to the environment. Wild yeast and bacteria naturally present in the air and on the grains settle into this mixture. As they multiply, they inoculate the starter.
- Fermentation: the wild yeast consumes the carbohydrates (sugars) in the flour, breaking them down into alcohol and carbon dioxide gas. The carbon dioxide gas gets trapped in the dough, causing it to rise and creating the airy crumb structure in sourdough bread.
- Acid Production: Simultaneously, the lactobacilli bacteria produce lactic and acetic acids through their metabolic processes. These acids give sourdough its signature tangy flavor, act as natural preservatives, and create a hostile environment for harmful bacteria.
- Flavor Development: Over time, the microbial community in the starter evolves and diversifies, resulting in a more complex flavor profile. This is why mature starters produce bread with a more nuanced taste compared to younger starters.

WHY IS SOURDOUGH STARTER SO SPECIAL?

Sourdough starters are special for several reasons:

- Cultural Heritage: Sourdough baking is deeply rooted in the history and traditions of various cultures. It has been passed down through generations, creating a sense of connection to the past and a shared culinary heritage.
- Flavor Complexity: Sourdough starters contribute to the complex and layered flavor profile of sourdough bread. The combination of lactic and acetic acids, along with aromatic compounds produced during fermentation, results in a unique taste experience.
- Digestibility: the long fermentation process in sourdough starter breaks down gluten and phytic acid, making the bread more digestible for some individuals with gluten sensitivities. It also has a lower glycemic index, which can help with blood sugar control.
- Versatility: Sourdough starters can be used to make a wide range of baked goods beyond bread, including pancakes, waffles, muffins, and more. The starter adds flavor, leavening, and a subtle tang to these creations.
- Low-Waste: Maintaining a sourdough starter is a sustainable practice. Instead of relying on store-bought yeast for every bake, you can continually feed and reuse your starter, reducing the need for packaged yeast.

Essential Tools and Ingredients

Sourdough baking is an art that has been cherished for centuries, and at the heart of this craft is the sourdough starter—a living ecosystem of wild yeast and lactic acid bacteria. Creating and maintaining a sourdough starter is the first step on your journey to making delicious, tangy sourdough bread. To embark on this culinary adventure, you'll need a few essential tools and ingredients. Let's explore them in detail.

TOOLS:

- Glass Jar or Container: A glass jar or food-safe plastic container with a lid is essential for creating and storing your sourdough starter. It should be large enough to accommodate the starter's growth, with some extra space at the top.
- Kitchen Scale: Accurate measurements are crucial in sourdough baking. A digital kitchen scale allows you to measure flour and water precisely, ensuring consistent results.
- Stirring Utensil: You'll need a utensil for stirring and feeding your starter. A wooden or silicone spatula or spoon is ideal because it won't react with the acidic environment of the starter.
- Rubber Band or Adhesive Tape: Use a rubber band or tape to mark the level of your starter in the jar. This helps you track its growth and determine when it's ready for use.
- Marker or Label: Label your jar with the date when you create your starter. This helps you keep track of its progress and know when it's time for feeding.
- Clean Towel or Cloth: A clean kitchen towel or cloth

can be used to cover your starter while it's resting. It allows air to circulate while preventing debris or insects from getting into the mixture.

INGREDIENTS:

- All-Purpose Flour: Unbleached all-purpose flour is commonly used to create and feed a sourdough starter. It provides the necessary carbohydrates for yeast and bacteria growth.
- Water: Chlorine-free, lukewarm water is essential for your starter. Chlorine can inhibit microbial growth, so use filtered or dechlorinated water. Ensure the water is at a temperature of around 70-75°F (21-24°C) to encourage yeast activity.
- Rye Flour (Optional): While all-purpose flour is the primary choice, some bakers prefer to kick-start their starter with a small amount of whole-grain rye flour. Rye flour contains natural yeast and bacteria that can help establish your starter more quickly.

The Science of Feeding Your Starter

Feeding your sourdough starter is not just a routine task; it's a fundamental aspect of sourdough baking that relies on the delicate interplay between flour, water, and a complex community of wild yeast and lactic acid bacteria. Understanding the science behind feeding your starter is key to maintaining its health and ensuring it produces the perfect rise and flavor in your sourdough bread. In this comprehensive exploration, we'll delve into the science of feeding your sourdough starter and the critical factors that come into play.

THE STARTER'S MICROBIAL COMMUNITY

Before we dive into the feeding process, let's get acquainted with the key players in your sourdough starter's microbial community:

- Wild Yeast (Saccharomyces cerevisiae): This is the primary leavening agent in your starter. Wild yeast ferments carbohydrates (sugars) in the flour, producing carbon dioxide gas, which creates the characteristic rise in sourdough bread. It also contributes to the flavor profile.
- Lactic Acid Bacteria (LAB): the LAB, primarily lactobacilli, are responsible for the sour flavor in sourdough. They produce lactic and acetic acids through fermentation. These acids not only add tanginess to the bread but also act as natural preservatives.
- Acetic Acid Bacteria (AAB): AAB contribute to the overall acidity and aroma of the sourdough starter. They produce acetic acid, which contributes to the sour taste and helps inhibit the growth of harmful bacteria.

FEEDING YOUR STARTER: THE BASICS

the process of feeding your sourdough starter involves discarding a portion of it and adding fresh flour and water. Let's break down the science behind each element of this process:

- Discarding: Discarding a portion of your starter serves several purposes:
- Reduction in Acid Load: Over time, the production of acids by LAB can build up, creating an overly acidic environment that inhibits yeast activity. Discarding a portion of the starter dilutes the acidity.
- Maintaining a Manageable Size: Starter can grow quickly, and keeping it at a manageable size ensures that you have enough space in your container and that it doesn't consume too much flour during feedings.
- Flour: Flour is the primary source of carbohydrates for the microbial community. As you add fresh flour to your starter, you're providing the microorganisms with new food to ferment. The carbohydrates in the flour are broken down into sugars, which the yeast and LAB feed on.
- Water: Water is crucial for creating the right consistency in your starter and ensuring that the flour is hydrated adequately. It also helps distribute the carbohydrates and minerals from the flour for microbial consumption.

THE FERMENTATION PROCESS

Feeding your starter initiates a new cycle of fermentation, and the microbial community gets to work on the fresh flour and water you've provided. Here's what happens during this process:

- Wild Yeast Activity: Wild yeast immediately begins to consume the carbohydrates in the fresh flour. As they metabolize these sugars, they produce carbon dioxide gas and alcohol. The gas gets trapped in the starter, causing it to rise.
- Acid Production: Lactic acid bacteria and acetic acid bacteria also become active. LAB produce lactic acid, contributing to the sour flavor, while AAB produce acetic acid, which adds another layer of tanginess.
- Flavor Development: the fermentation process is not just about leavening; it's also about flavor development. During fermentation, the microbial community produces a wide range of volatile organic compounds, including esters, aldehydes, and ketones, which contribute to the unique aroma and flavor of sourdough.
- Microbial Competition: In a healthy starter, the wild yeast and LAB outcompete harmful microorganisms. The acidic environment created by the acids they produce helps inhibit the growth of undesirable bacteria.
- Microbial Symbiosis: Wild yeast and LAB have a symbiotic relationship. The yeast produces alcohol, which the LAB convert into lactic and acetic acids. This symbiosis is critical for maintaining a healthy starter.

HYDRATION LEVEL AND CONSISTENCY

the hydration level of your starter refers to the ratio of water to flour. The consistency of your starter—whether it's thick like dough or more like a batter—depends on its hydration level. Understanding hydration is essential for feeding your starter correctly:

- High Hydration (Batter-Like): A high-hydration starter has a higher ratio of water to flour (usually around 100% hydration or more). It has a thinner, batter-like consistency. High-hydration starters tend to ferment more quickly and produce a milder sour flavor.
- Low Hydration (Dough-Like): A low-hydration starter has a lower ratio of water to flour (typically around 60-75% hydration). It has a thicker, dough-like consistency. Low-hydration starters ferment more slowly and often develop a more pronounced sour flavor.
- the choice of hydration level depends on your personal preference and the type of bread you want to bake. Some bakers maintain multiple starters with different hydration levels for versatility.

THE IMPORTANCE OF TEMPERATURE

Temperature plays a significant role in the fermentation process. Here's how it affects your starter:

- Fermentation Rate: Higher temperatures accelerate fermentation, while lower temperatures slow it down. A warmer environment can lead to faster rise times and more pronounced sourness, while cooler temperatures result in milder flavors.
- Microbial Activity: Different temperatures favor the growth of specific microorganisms. Wild yeast is more active at warmer temperatures, while LAB thrive in slightly cooler conditions. Finding the right balance of temperature for your starter's desired characteristics is key.
- Maintaining Consistency: Consistency in temperature is crucial for predictable results. Sudden fluctuations in temperature can affect the microbial balance in your starter.

TROUBLESHOOTING FEEDING ISSUES

Feeding your starter may not always go smoothly, and it's important to troubleshoot common issues:

- Slow Activity: If your starter's rise and fall times are inconsistent or too slow, try adjusting the temperature, flour type, or hydration level to better suit the microorganisms' needs.
- Overly Acidic: If your starter becomes overly acidic, reducing the feeding frequency or increasing the amount of fresh flour in each feeding can help dilute the acidity.
- Inconsistent Rise: Inconsistencies in your starter's rise and fall may result from inconsistent feeding ratios or temperature fluctuations. Ensure that you maintain a consistent routine.
- Stagnant Growth: If your starter appears stuck and doesn't show signs of fermentation, it may need more frequent feedings or a different flour type to provide a fresh source of nutrients.

- Mold or Off Odors: Mold growth or unpleasant odors may indicate contamination. In such cases, it's best to discard your starter and start fresh.

Creating and Maintaining Your Starter

Creating and maintaining a sourdough starter is a journey that combines the simplicity of two primary ingredients, flour and water, with the complexity of a living ecosystem of wild yeast and bacteria. This humble mixture, when nurtured and fed with care, becomes the heart and soul of sourdough bread baking. In this comprehensive guide, we will take you through the process of creating your sourdough starter from scratch and provide you with the essential steps to maintain its health and vitality.

CREATING YOUR SOURDOUGH STARTER

DAY 1: THE BEGINNING

- Choose Your Flour: You can start your sourdough journey with all-purpose flour, whole wheat flour, or a mixture of both. All-purpose flour is a common choice for beginners due to its balanced gluten content.
- Mix Flour and Water: In a clean glass jar or food-safe plastic container, combine 4 ounces (approximately 1/2 cup) of flour and 4 ounces (about 1/2 cup) of lukewarm, chlorine-free water. Stir vigorously until the mixture forms a thick, paste-like consistency. Ensure that there are no dry pockets of flour.
- Cover and Rest: Cover the container loosely with a clean kitchen towel or plastic wrap. Let it rest at room temperature (around 70-75°F or 21-24°C) for 24 hours. This initial resting period allows wild yeast and bacteria from the environment to begin colonizing your mixture.

DAY 2: THE FIRST FEEDING
- Check for Bubbles: After 24 hours, check for signs of fermentation. You may notice small bubbles forming on the surface of your mixture. If you do, that's a positive sign that the wild yeast is starting to become active.
- Discard and Feed: Regardless of whether you see bubbles, it's time for your first feeding. Discard half of the mixture (about 4 ounces) and add 4 ounces each of fresh flour and lukewarm water. Mix thoroughly until well combined.
- Cover and Rest: Cover the container again and let it rest for another 24 hours.

DAYS 3-7: CONSISTENT FEEDING
- Repeat the Feeding: Continue the daily feeding routine by discarding half of the mixture and adding 4 ounces each of fresh flour and water. Over the course of these days, you should observe increasing signs of fermentation, including more bubbles and a slightly tangy aroma.
- Look for Consistency: By the end of the first week, your sourdough starter should be consistently bubbling and increasing in volume after each feeding. It may have a pleasant sour aroma. You've now created a basic starter.

DAY 7: YOUR SOURDOUGH STARTER IS BORN
- Mature Starter: Congratulations! Your sourdough starter is mature and ready to use for baking. It should have a robust microbial community, which will continue to evolve over time, enhancing its flavor complexity.

MAINTAINING YOUR SOURDOUGH STARTER
Now that you have successfully created your sourdough starter, it's essential to maintain its health and vitality. Follow these steps for regular upkeep:

DAILY OR WEEKLY FEEDING:
- Choose a Feeding Schedule: Depending on your baking frequency, you can choose to feed your starter daily or weekly. Daily feedings are typical for active bakers, while weekly feedings are suitable for occasional bakers.
- Discard and Feed: Before feeding, discard a portion of your starter. This prevents it from accumulating and becoming too large. You can either discard half or a specific amount, depending on your preference.
- Feed with Fresh Flour and Water: Add equal parts (by weight) of flour and water to the remaining starter. Stir well to combine. Maintain a consistent ratio of flour to water to keep your starter at your desired hydration level.
- Resting Temperature: Keep your starter at room temperature between feedings if you're baking frequently. If you're not baking for an extended period, you can store it in the refrigerator and feed it weekly.
- Monitoring: Pay attention to your starter's activity. It should continue to rise and fall predictably after feedings. A mature starter should have a pleasant, slightly tangy aroma.

- Maintain Consistency: Consistency is key in sourdough maintenance. Use the same type of flour and water for feedings, and maintain a regular feeding schedule to keep your starter healthy.

REVIVING A DORMANT STARTER:
If you've stored your starter in the refrigerator and it hasn't been fed for a while, you can easily revive it:

- Take It Out: Remove your starter from the refrigerator and let it sit at room temperature for a few hours to activate.
- Discard and Feed: Discard a portion of your starter, leaving about 4 ounces. Feed it with equal parts fresh flour and water. Repeat this process daily until your starter is consistently active and ready for baking.

TROUBLESHOOTING YOUR SOURDOUGH STARTER
Creating and maintaining a sourdough starter is a relatively straightforward process, but it can sometimes encounter challenges:

- Slow Activity: If your starter is not showing much activity, be patient. It can take a bit longer to become established. Continue with regular feedings, and it should improve over time.
- Off Odors: If your starter develops unpleasant odors, it may indicate that bad bacteria have taken over. In this case, start a new starter from scratch.
- Mold Growth: Mold can occasionally appear on the surface of a starter. To prevent this, maintain good hygiene, and keep your container clean. If mold appears, discard the affected portion and feed the remaining starter.
- Separation: Sometimes, your starter may separate into liquid and solid layers. This is normal, especially for high-hydration starters. Simply stir it back together during feeding.
- Inconsistent Rising: If your starter's rise and fall are inconsistent, try adjusting the feeding ratio or the feeding frequency to better suit its needs.
- Remember that sourdough starters are adaptable and can recover from many setbacks with patience and care. Each starter has its unique personality and may behave differently based on the environment, flour type, and hydration level.

Chapter 3

Breakfast Goodies

Scallion Pancakes

Prep time: 10 minutes | Cook time: 40 minutes | Makes
6 Pancakes

Scallion pancakes, known for their crispy exterior and layers of savory goodness, are a beloved staple in Asian cuisine. Imagine biting into a pancake that's both tender and flaky, with bursts of fresh scallion flavor in every mouthful. These pancakes are a culinary delight, whether enjoyed as an appetizer, side dish, or even a light meal.

Scallion pancakes are characterized by their unique combination of textures. The exterior is wonderfully crisp and golden, while the inside remains tender and chewy. The addition of chopped scallions lends a delightful freshness and a hint of mild onion flavor to each bite.

Pair these scallion pancakes with a simple soy-based dipping sauce or a tangy vinegar dip for a perfect harmony of flavors. They also pair well with various Asian dishes, such as stir-fries, soups, or as a side to complement the richness of grilled meats.

Crafting scallion pancakes involves a simple yet satisfying process. The dough, made from flour and water, is rolled out and generously sprinkled with chopped scallions before being folded, rolled, and pan-fried to perfection.Scallion pancakes are a testament to the beauty of simplicity in Asian cuisine, offering a delectable experience that's sure to become a favorite.

Pancake Dough:
- 240 g (2 cups) all-purpose flour
- 60 g (½ cup) cornstarch
- 3 g (½ tsp) Chinese five-spice powder
- 3 g (½ tsp) salt
- 56 g (¼ cup) sourdough discard
- 113 g (½ cup) boiling water

- 14 g (1 tbsp) toasted sesame oil
- 56 g (¼ cup) melted lard or vegetable oil
- 3 scallions, thinly sliced
- 56 to 84 g (4 to 6 tbsp) vegetable oil

Dipping Sauce:
- 28 g (2 tbsp) soy sauce
- 1 scallion, thinly sliced
- 8 g (2 tsp) rice vinegar
- 4 g (1 tsp) honey
- 4 g (1 tsp) toasted sesame oil
- pinch of red pepper flakes

1. Whisk together the flour, cornstarch, five-spice powder and salt in a large mixing bowl until no lumps remain. Work the wet ingredients into the flour mixture until everything is fully combined and forms a dough. Cover the bowl with a damp kitchen towel and allow the dough to rest for 15 minutes.
2. Knead the dough for 5 to 10 minutes until it's extremely smooth and pliable. Return the dough to the bowl and cover with the kitchen towel. Allow the dough to rest for another 30 minutes. This rest period will let the gluten relax and will make it easier to roll out the dough.
3. While you're waiting, make the dipping sauce. In a small serving bowl, combine the soy sauce, scallion, vinegar, honey, sesame oil and red pepper flakes.
4. Divide the dough into six equal portions. Flatten each piece of dough and then roll it into a large round circle; rolling the dough as thin as possible will result in flakier pancakes.Use your hands to flatten each piece into a 15-cm disk about ⅛ inch 3 mm thick.
5. Heat 1 tablespoon 15 ml of vegetable oil in a small skillet over medium-high heat. Cook one pancake at a time until it's golden brown, about 2 to 3 minutes on each side.

Potato Rolls

Prep time: 55 minutes | Cook time: 20 minutes | Makes 24 pieces

Potato rolls are a delightful twist on the classic bread roll, adding a touch of homey comfort to any meal. Imagine the scent of freshly baked bread filling your kitchen, the anticipation of that first warm, soft bite. These potato rolls bring that experience to your table.

these rolls are distinguished by their plush, tender crumb and a subtle earthy flavor contributed by the potatoes. The addition of mashed potatoes to the dough not only adds moisture but also creates a unique texture and flavor profile.

Pair these potato rolls with soups, stews, or sandwiches. They're ideal for sliders, pulled pork, or even as burger buns. Serve them with a dollop of butter or your favorite spreads for a delightful snack.

Making potato rolls is a rewarding culinary adventure. You'll start by preparing a simple dough, incorporating mashed potatoes for that distinctive texture. The result? A batch of soft, pillowy rolls that will elevate any meal and leave everyone at your table craving for more.

- 2 sweet potatoes, cooked, peeled, and mashed
- 240 ml milk
- 45 g butter, softened
- 480 g white flour
- 1 egg, whisked
- 5 g salt
- 10 g dry yeast

1. In your bread machine, combine the mashed sweet potatoes, milk, white flour, softened butter, whisked egg, salt, and dry yeast. Use the "Basil" or similar dough cycle on your bread machine.
2. Once the dough cycle is complete, tear pieces of the dough and shape them into medium-sized balls.
3. Arrange the dough balls on a lined baking sheet, leaving some space between them.
4. Allow the dough balls to rise for about 45 minutes in a warm place.
5. Preheat your oven to 375 degrees F (190 degrees C).
6. Bake the risen dough balls in the preheated oven for approximately 20 minutes or until they are golden brown.
7. Remove the sweet potato rolls from the oven and let them cool slightly on a wire rack.

Bacon and Cheese Biscuits

Prep time: 10 minutes | Cook time: 20 minutes | Makes 10 to 12 biscuits

Bacon and Cheese Biscuits are the epitome of savory indulgence. Picture golden-brown, flaky biscuits fresh from the oven, oozing with melted cheese and boasting the irresistible aroma of crispy bacon. These biscuits are a culinary masterpiece that combines smoky, salty, and cheesy goodness into one delightful package.

these biscuits are the ultimate comfort food. The smoky and savory notes from the bacon perfectly complement the richness of the melted cheese, while the biscuit's flaky layers provide a satisfying crunch. Their versatility shines through as they can serve as a hearty breakfast, a savory side dish, or a delectable snack.

Creating these biscuits is a straightforward yet rewarding endeavor. Start by preparing a simple biscuit dough, then fold in crispy bacon bits and shredded cheese. Bacon and Cheese Biscuits are a treat worth savoring.

- 240 grams unbleached all-purpose flour
- 10 grams baking powder
- 2.5 grams baking soda
- 1.25 grams salt
- 75 grams very cold butter, cubed
- 75 grams shredded cheddar cheese
- 8 slices bacon, cooked, cooled, and crumbled
- 240 milliliters active starter

1. Preheat the oven to 220°C (425°F). Line a baking sheet with a silicone baking mat or parchment paper; set it aside.
2. In a medium mixing bowl, whisk together the flour, baking powder, baking soda, and salt.
3. Using a pastry cutter or fork, mix in the cold butter until the mixture resembles coarse crumbs. Work quickly to prevent the butter from getting too warm.
4. Mix in the cheese and crumbled bacon.
5. Next, add 180 milliliters (¾ cup) of the active starter and mix until a soft dough forms. If needed, add the remaining starter to achieve the desired consistency.
6. Turn out the dough onto a floured work surface and gently knead it a few times. Using your hands or a rolling pin, flatten the dough to a thickness of about 2.5 centimeters (1 inch).
7. Place the biscuits on the prepared baking sheet and bake for 12 to 15 minutes, or until they are puffed and golden.

Cornbread

Prep time: 10 minutes | Cook time: 20 minutes | Serves 6 to 8

Cornbread is a quintessential Southern classic that embodies the warm embrace of comfort food. Imagine a slice of golden, slightly sweet, crumbly goodness, melting in your mouth with every bite. Cornbread is more than just a side dish; it's a cherished tradition passed down through generations, a symbol of Southern hospitality, and a testament to the rich flavors of the American South.

Cornbread is celebrated for its unique texture and taste, which come from the combination of cornmeal, flour, and a hint of sweetness. The contrast between its crispy, buttery crust and the soft, moist interior is simply irresistible. Its versatility is another hallmark, as it pairs seamlessly with a wide range of dishes, from spicy chili to succulent barbecue.

Serve warm slices of cornbread as a side to complement hearty dishes like chili, gumbo, or fried chicken. It also shines as a standalone snack, spread with a pat of butter or drizzled with honey. For a sweet twist, try it with fruit preserves or alongside a bowl of comforting soup.

Making cornbread is relatively straightforward, requiring just a handful of pantry staples. Mix cornmeal, flour, leavening agents, and a touch of sugar, then combine with buttermilk and eggs for moisture and richness. The batter is poured into a hot skillet or baking dish, creating that iconic crispy edge. The result is a soul-warming delight that embodies the essence of Southern cuisine.

Cornbread isn't just a bread; it's a cherished part of the Southern culinary heritage.

- 240 grams starter (discard is fine)
- 240 milliliters buttermilk
- 120 grams cornmeal
- 120 grams unbleached all-purpose flour
- 2 eggs
- 115 grams butter, melted and cooled but still liquid
- 50 grams sugar
- 2.5 grams salt
- 5 grams baking powder
- 2.5 grams baking soda

1. In a medium mixing bowl, mix the starter, buttermilk, cornmeal, and flour. You can cover the bowl with plastic wrap and set it aside at room temperature for an hour or two to further develop flavor, or continue immediately with the next steps.
2. Preheat the oven to 175°C (350°F). Generously grease or butter a 9-inch cast-iron skillet, deep dish pie plate, or baking dish, and set it aside while you finish mixing the batter.
3. To the flour mixture, add the eggs, melted butter, sugar, and salt, and stir to combine. Add the baking powder and baking soda, then stir again.
4. Place the batter into the prepared baking container and smooth the top of the batter.
5. Bake for 35 to 40 minutes or until the cornbread is light brown on top and the middle is cooked through.
6. Allow the cornbread to cool for about 10 minutes before slicing.

Rye Pancakes

Prep time: 10 minutes | Cook time: 20 minutes | Makes 10 to 12 pancakes

Rye pancakes are a delightful twist on the classic breakfast favorite, adding a rustic and nutty flavor to your morning routine. Picture a stack of golden-brown pancakes, their aroma wafting through the kitchen, promising a comforting and satisfying start to your day.

these pancakes are a hearty alternative to traditional buttermilk pancakes, thanks to the inclusion of rye flour. Rye imparts a unique earthy flavor, along with a slightly denser texture that many find incredibly satisfying. The nutty undertones of rye complement sweet or savory toppings, making them a versatile choice for breakfast.

Serve these rye pancakes with a dollop of Greek yogurt and a drizzle of honey for a healthy and indulgent breakfast. Rye pancakes also make a fantastic base for fruit compotes or preserves.

Creating rye pancakes is a straightforward process. The batter consists of rye flour, all-purpose flour, baking powder, eggs, and milk. Enjoy them as a delightful departure from ordinary pancakes, infusing your breakfast with wholesome goodness.

- 480 g active starter
- 1 egg, beaten
- 120 g milk
- 30 g butter, melted and cooled slightly
- 25 g granulated sugar
- 6 g salt
- 115 g rye flour
- unbleached all-purpose flour as needed
- ½ tsp. baking soda dissolved in 1 t. water

1. In a medium mixing bowl, stir together the starter, egg, milk, butter, sugar, and salt until well combined. Add the rye flour and stir again; add enough all-purpose flour to attain the desired pancake batter consistency. Mix thoroughly so there are no lumps in the batter. Right before ready to begin cooking, pour in the dissolved baking soda and mix thoroughly again.
2. Pour ¼ cup batter per pancake into a heated and greased pan or skillet and cook for about 3 minutes; flip the pancakes and cook the second side until done (about 2 minutes).
3. Serve with butter, syrup, jam, or sweetened applesauce.

Hamburger Buns

Prep time: 10 minutes | Cook time: 20 minutes | Serves 4

Hamburger buns are the unsung heroes of the burger world, providing the Picture a burger joint where the buns are made fresh daily, boasting a golden, slightly crisp exterior and a soft, pillowy interior that cradles your favorite burger creation.

these buns are all about providing the best possible burger experience. chosen toppings while adding a subtle richness of their own.

Pair these hamburger buns with anything from classic beef burgers to veggie or chicken alternatives. Whether you're grilling in the backyard or assembling sliders for a party, these buns will elevate your burger game.

Making hamburger buns at home is a rewarding endeavor.So, get ready to take your burger nights to the next level with these delectable buns as your foundation for burger bliss.

- 430 grams unbleached all-purpose flour, divided
- 240 milliliters milk, slightly warm
- 60 grams active starter
- 2 eggs, divided
- 2 teaspoons granulated sugar
- 1 teaspoon active dry yeast
- 1 teaspoon salt
- 3 teaspoons butter, softened to room temperature
- 2 teaspoons sesame seeds (optional)

1. In a stand mixer with a dough hook, combine 300 grams of the flour with the milk, starter, 1 of the eggs, sugar, yeast, and salt. Beat on low to medium speed until a shaggy dough forms. Cover the mixture with a damp cloth or plastic wrap and let the dough rest for 30 minutes.
2. Still using the dough hook, knead the dough for 7 to 8 minutes, gradually adding the remainder of the flour interspersed with pieces of the butter. The dough should be soft and sticky but able to pull away from the sides of the bowl.
3. Using a spatula or dough scraper, turn out the dough into a large, greased mixing bowl. Cover the bowl with plastic wrap and let it rest at room temperature for 2 to 3 hours or until the dough is about doubled in bulk.

Overnight Mini Sourdough English Muffins

Prep time: 5 minutes | Cook time: 15 minutes | Makes 10 to 12 mini English muffins

Overnight mini sourdough English muffins are a delightful twist on a classic breakfast favorite. Imagine waking up to the aroma of freshly baked, golden-brown muffins, each one boasting the tangy and complex flavor of sourdough. These bite-sized wonders are perfect for a leisurely breakfast or brunch, and they're sure to elevate your morning routine.

Crafted with a sourdough starter, these mini muffins feature all the wonderful characteristics of traditional English muffins – nooks and crannies for absorbing butter or jam, a satisfying chewiness, and a hint of sourness that adds depth to their flavor profile.

Pair these mini sourdough English muffins with your favorite spreads like butter, cream cheese, or homemade fruit preserves. They're also an excellent foundation for breakfast sandwiches, making them a versatile addition to your morning menu.

- 245 g (1 cup plus 1 tsp) milk, whole or 2%
- 120 g (½ cup) water
- 56 g (4 tbsp) unsalted butter, cubed
- 75 g (heaped ⅓ cup) bubbly, active starter
- 24 g (2 tbsp) sugar
- 500 g (4 cups plus 2 tbsp) all-purpose flour
- 9 g (1½ tsp) salt
- cornmeal or semolina flour, for dusting

Make the Dough:
1. In a small saucepan, warm the milk, water, and butter together over low heat or in the microwave. Cool slightly before adding to the dough.
2. After the dough has rested, work the mass into a semi-smooth ball, about 15 to 20 seconds.

Bulk Rise:
1. Cover the bowl with a damp towel and let rise until double in size, about 8 to 10 hours at 21°C. Once fully risen, cover the dough in lightly oiled plastic wrap and chill it overnight.

Shape:
1. In the morning, remove the cold dough onto a floured work surface and let rest for 10 minutes. Line a sheet pan with parchment paper and sprinkle generously with cornmeal to prevent sticking.
2. with floured hands, pat the dough into a rectangle or oval shape, about 1.25 cm thick. Place the rounds onto your sheet pan and sprinkle the tops with cornmeal.

Second Rise:
1. Cover the dough with a damp towel and let rest until puffy, about 1 hour, depending on temperature.

Cook the Muffins:
1. Warm a large nonstick skillet over low heat. Place a few rounds of dough into the pan to fit comfortably; they do not spread very much when cooking. Back when pressed gently.
2. These English muffins will stay fresh up to 2 days, stored in a plastic bag at room temperature.

Apple and Apricot Enriched Sourdough "Roses"

Prep time: 10 minutes | Cook time: 1 hour 5 minutes | Serves 12

Apple and apricot enriched sourdough "roses" are a visual and culinary masterpiece that combines the artistry of baking with the natural sweetness of fruit. Picture a platter adorned with delicate rose-shaped pastries, each one crafted from layers of soft, tangy sourdough and filled with the vibrant flavors of apples and apricots. These edible "roses" are not just a treat for the taste buds but also a feast for the eyes.

these pastries are a fusion of artisanal sourdough and the sweetness of fruit, resulting in a complex flavor profile that's both satisfying and refined. The sourdough layers provide a subtle tanginess, which perfectly complements the natural sweetness of apples and apricots. The visual appeal of these "roses" makes them an impressive choice for special occasions or simply for indulging in a moment of culinary artistry.

Pair these apple and apricot enriched sourdough "roses" with a dusting of powdered sugar for a touch of elegance or a drizzle of honey to enhance the fruity sweetness. They're equally delicious served warm or at room temperature, making them suitable for brunch, dessert, or an afternoon tea.

Creating these "roses" is a labor of love, as it involves layering and rolling the sourdough with apple and apricot fillings. The result is a batch of pastries that not only taste exquisite but also showcase the skill and creativity of the baker. With each bite, you'll savor the balance of textures and flavors, making these "roses" a true delight for both the palate and the senses.

- 30 g (⅛ cup) active starter
- 200 g (¾ cup) milk, cold or at room temperature (I use reduced-fat or 2% milk, but you can also use full-fat/whole milk)
- 1 large egg
- 30 g (⅛ cup) salted butter, at room temperature
- 30 g (⅛ cup) runny honey
- 400 g (3⅛ cups) strong white bread flour
- 7 g (1 tsp) salt, or to taste

Filling:
- 3 small, sweet, red apples, peeled (100 g [3½ oz]) (I use Royal Gala apples)
- 100 g (½ cup) apricot jam
- 10 g (2 tsp) lemon juice, to prepare apples

Topping:
- Granulated sugar, vanilla or cinnamon sugar to sprinkle on top, optional

1. In the early evening, in a large mixing bowl, roughly mix together all the ingredients, except the fillings and optional topping. It will be a ragged dough, and it may be easier to use a bowl scraper or spatula to mix it at this stage. The butter will not be fully mixed through yet; it will become mixed in fully as you complete the next steps. Cover the bowl with a clean shower cap or your choice of cover and leave the bowl on the counter.
2. After 2 hours, perform the first set of pulls and folds on the dough, lifting and pulling the dough across the bowl until it starts to come into a soft ball, then stop. The butter will still not be fully mixed in yet, but will become more so as you work with the dough. During this first set of pulls and folds, the dough may still be sticky and quite stiff but stretchable.
3. Cover the bowl again and leave it to sit on the counter.
4. After 1 to 1½ hours, perform another set of pulls and folds on the dough. The dough will remain slightly sticky but will be nicely stretchy and will come together into a soft, smooth ball.
5. Leave the covered bowl on the counter overnight, typically 8 to 12 hours, at 18 to 20°C.
6. In the morning, hopefully the dough will have grown to between double and triple in size, with a smooth surface. If the dough does not seem sufficiently proofed yet, allow it a few more hours to continue to proof. This is a heavy dough and may take longer than a standard water-based dough to fully proof.
7. Place the dough, untouched but still covered, in the fridge for at least an hour, until you are ready to use it. The dough will firm up, making it easier to work with later.

Cherry & Almond Bake

Prep time: 5 minutes | Cook time: 10 minutes | Makes 1 30cm bake

the Cherry & Almond Bake is a delightful dessert that marries the natural sweetness of cherries with the rich, nutty flavor of almonds. Imagine a warm, golden-brown casserole bubbling with juicy cherries and crowned with a generous layer of almond-studded crumble. This dessert is an ode to the harmonious pairing of fruit and nuts.

the starring ingredients in this dessert are the plump, juicy cherries, which burst with flavor as they bake, creating a luscious filling that's both tart and sweet. The almond-infused crumble topping adds a delightful crunch and a toasty, nutty richness that perfectly complements the cherries.

Pair this Cherry & Almond Bake with a scoop of vanilla ice cream or a dollop of whipped cream for a heavenly dessert experience. The contrast of the warm, fruity filling and the cold, creamy accompaniment is simply divine.

Creating this dessert is a straightforward process. You'll start by preparing the cherry filling, layering it in a baking dish, and then topping it with a crumble mixture made from almonds, flour, sugar, and butter. The Cherry & Almond Bake is a comforting and irresistible dessert that embodies the essence of homemade goodness.

- 100g organic stoneground wholegrain flour (11.5% protein)
- 75g plain flour
- 3 large free-range eggs, at room temperature
- 175g sunflower oil, plus extra for greasing
- 175g caster sugar
- 2 tablespoons dried rose petals
- 1 tablespoon vanilla extract
- 175g bubbly, lively second-build starter
- 100g fresh cherries, halved and stoned
- 2 tablespoons (20–25g) flaked almonds

MIX:

1. Put all the except the cherries and almonds into a large mixing bowl and combine to form a loose batter – it might seem too wet, but don't worry. After you remove the starter to use in the dough, refresh the remaining starter in your jar and put to one side.

PROVE:

2. Grease a 30cm, 3cm deep flan tin and line with baking parchment. Pour the batter into the tin, then leave somewhere warm (about 28–30°C) to prove overnight – perhaps in an airing cupboard or in the oven with just the light on. (the batter needs this warmth to prove because the oil, sugar and eggs have an osmotic effect on the yeast.)

BAKE:

3. the next morning, preheat your oven to 180°C/gas mark 4. Scatter the cherries and almonds over the top of the cake and bake for about 20–25 minutes until the sponge is tender, golden and light and a skewer inserted into the middle comes out clean. Cool for 5 minutes in the tin, then remove from the tin and transfer to a wire rack to cool completely.
4. By now, your starter should be ready to put in the fridge until you next want to prepare it for baking.
5. the bake will keep for a few days. I usually slice it, then wrap each slice in greaseproof paper and store in a tin.

Hummus & Olive Flatbread

Prep time: 5 minutes | Cook time: 10 minutes | Makes 1 large flatbread

Hummus & Olive Flatbread is a Mediterranean-inspired delight that brings together the creamy, savory richness of hummus with the briny, earthy flavors of olives on a canvas of perfectly baked flatbread. Imagine a sheet of golden, crispy dough topped with velvety hummus, scattered with vibrant olives, and garnished with aromatic herbs—a symphony of Mediterranean flavors and textures.

This dish combines the silky smoothness of hummus with the salty and complex taste of olives, offering a unique blend of creaminess and crunch. The flatbread serves as a sturdy foundation, ensuring each bite is a harmonious explosion of flavors.

Pair this Hummus & Olive Flatbread with a drizzle of high-quality olive oil and a sprinkle of fresh herbs for a touch of Mediterranean elegance. It's an ideal appetizer, snack, or even a light meal, making it versatile for any occasion.

Creating this flatbread is a straightforward process. You'll start by preparing or purchasing flatbread as your base. Spread a generous layer of hummus on top, and then scatter a variety of olives for a visually appealing and flavorful topping. Hummus & Olive Flatbread is an invitation to savor the beauty of Mediterranean flavors in every bite.

- 360g water at 27°C
- 100g bubbly, lively second-build starter
- 350g organic white flour (13% protein)
- 150g organic stoneground wholegrain flour (11.5% protein)
- 10g fine sea salt, plus extra for sprinkling
- 100g hummus
- olive oil, for greasing and drizzling
- 1 tablespoon polenta, for dusting
- 20 green olives, pitted

MIX:

1. In a large bowl, whisk together 350g of the water and the sourdough starter. Refresh the remaining starter in your jar and put to one side.
2. Add the flours and salt to the bowl and mix vigorously using a strong spatula for about 2 minutes. It will form a stiff ball. Leave to rest for 30 minutes, then mix in the remaining 10g water using the bassinage technique described . This should take less than 1 minute.

PROVE:

3. Lightly grease a 23cm cake tin. Place your dough in the tin, cover and leave to prove on the kitchen table to prove.

BAKE:

4. By morning, your loaf will be at least 50 per cent bigger. Preheat your oven to 220°C/gas mark 7. When you turn the oven on to preheat, place a baking sheet in the oven to heat up for 30 minutes, and place a shallow baking tray in the bottom of the oven.
5. Take the hot baking sheet out of the oven and sprinkle it with the polenta. Turn your dough out on to the baking sheet. As you place the flatbread in the oven, carefully throw a little water or some ice cubes into the hot tray at the bottom. Close the door quickly to trap the steam this creates. Bake for 18–20 minutes until it's beautifully golden.
6. Remove the flatbread from the oven and leave to cool on a wire rack. Your starter should now be ready to put in the fridge until you next want to prepare it for baking.

Garam Masala Spelt Tin Loaf

Prep time: 5 minutes | Cook time: 10 minutes | Makes 1 large loaf (900g/2lb loaf tin)

The Garam Masala Spelt Tin Loaf is a unique and aromatic bread that harmoniously blends the warm, exotic flavors of garam masala with the wholesome goodness of spelt flour. Picture a rustic tin loaf, emerging from the oven with a tantalizing aroma that combines the rich spices of garam masala with the nutty sweetness of spelt. This bread is a celebration of culinary fusion.

At the heart of this loaf is the enchanting fragrance and complexity of garam masala—a blend of warm spices like cinnamon, cardamom, and cloves. These spices infuse the bread with a deep, earthy warmth that's balanced by the nutty, slightly sweet notes of spelt flour.

Pair this Garam Masala Spelt Tin Loaf with a smear of creamy goat cheese or enjoy it alongside your favorite Indian or Middle Eastern dishes. Its unique flavor profile makes it a versatile companion for both savory and sweet accompaniments.

Crafting this tin loaf involves the art of bread baking and spice blending. The spelt flour and garam masala are meticulously combined to create a dough that's

as aromatic as it is nutritious. After rising, the dough is gently shaped into a tin loaf, allowing it to develop its unique texture and flavor. The Garam Masala Spelt Tin Loaf is a testament to the creative possibilities of bread making, offering a delicious journey of flavors that transcend borders and cultures.

- 375g water at 27°C
- 100g bubbly, lively second-build starter
- 250g organic stoneground wholegrain spelt flour
- 250g organic white flour (13% protein)
- 10g fine sea salt
- 1 generous tablespoon ghee, at room temperature
- 1 heaped tablespoon garam masala

MIX:

1. In a large bowl, whisk together 350g of the water and the sourdough starter. Refresh the remaining starter in your jar and put to one side.
2. Add the flours and salt to the bowl and mix vigorously using a strong spatula for about 2 minutes. It will form a stiff ball. Leave to rest for 30 minutes, then mix in the remaining 25g water using the bassinage technique described . This should take less than 1 minute. Cover and leave the dough to rest for another 30 minutes.

PROVE:

3. Generously grease the inside of a 900g (2lb) loaf tin with the ghee and dust with the garam masala. Place the dough into the greased tin. Cover and leave to prove on the kitchen table overnight.

BAKE:

4. The following morning, your loaf will be at least 50 per cent bigger. Preheat your oven to 220°C/gas mark 7 for 30 minutes, and place a shallow baking tray in the bottom of the oven.
5. As you place the bread in the oven, reduce the temperature to 180°C/gas mark 4 and carefully throw a little water or some ice cubes into the hot tray at the bottom. Your starter should now be ready to put in the fridge until you next want to prepare it for baking.
6. Once cool, store your loaf wrapped in a clean, dry tea towel. Best enjoyed within 2–3 days. This is delicious with cheese and chutney or ham.

Fennel Fougasse

Prep time: 5 minutes | Cook time: 10 minutes | Makes 1 large bake (37 x 27cm)

The Fennel Fougasse is a masterpiece of bread craftsmanship, combining the rustic elegance of a traditional fougasse with the aromatic allure of fennel seeds. Imagine a loaf that resembles a leaf or an ear of wheat, intricately slashed and adorned with fragrant fennel seeds, creating a visual and sensory feast. This artisanal bread is a testament to the craftsmanship of French baking.

The Fennel Fougasse features a golden-brown crust that gives way to a tender and airy crumb. Its flavor is a delightful dance of nuttiness from the bread itself and the warm, earthy notes of fennel seeds. This bread is perfect as a standalone snack or as a charming accompaniment to soups, salads, and charcuterie boards.

Pair this Fennel Fougasse with a drizzle of high-quality olive oil or balsamic reduction for a sophisticated appetizer, or enjoy it as a complement to savory spreads and cheeses. Its artisanal appearance makes it a centerpiece at any gathering.

Creating a Fennel Fougasse is a blend of art and science. The dough is prepared with attention to detail, allowing it to rise and develop flavor and texture. It's then shaped into the distinct fougasse form, featuring intricate slashes and a generous scattering of fennel seeds. As it bakes, the bread transforms into a stunning centerpiece that not only captivates The eye but also seduces the palate with its complex flavors and textures. The Fennel Fougasse is a testament to the beauty of French baking, a sensory experience that invites you to savor the artistry of breadmaking.

- 375g water at 27°C
- 100g bubbly, lively second-build starter
- 250g organic white flour (13% protein)
- 10g fine sea salt
- olive oil spray
- 1 heaped tablespoon fennel seeds
- small bunch of fresh fennel leaves, roughly chopped

MIX:

1. In a large mixing bowl, whisk together 350g of the water and the sourdough starter. Add the flours and salt to the mixing bowl and use a strong spatula to vigorously stir the until they are completely combined and there is no dry flour remaining. This should take about 2 minutes. Leave to rest for 30 minutes. Meanwhile, refresh the remaining starter in your jar and set aside.

2. Add the remaining 25g water to the dough using the bassinage technique described and mix for a further 1 minute to incorporate.

PROVE:

3. Cover the bowl and leave to prove on the kitchen table overnight.

BAKE:

4. Spray a 37 x 27cm baking tin with olive oil. If you like, you can line it with baking parchment and then spray with oil. Preheat your oven to 220°C/gas mark 7 for 30 minutes and place a shallow baking tray in the bottom of the oven.

5. Give the surface of the dough a generous spray with olive oil and place it in the prepared baking tin. Using your fingertips, gently push the dough outwards to cover the base of the tin. Leave to rest for 1 minute.

Rose, Coconut & Raspberry Cake

Prep time: 5 minutes | Cook time: 10 minutes | Makes 1 large cake (serves 12 generously)

The Rose, Coconut & Raspberry Cake is a confectionery masterpiece that brings together the delicate floral notes of rosewater, the tropical sweetness of coconut, and the vibrant tartness of raspberries. This cake is not only a visual delight but also a harmonious fusion of flavors and textures.

The centerpiece of this cake is the subtle and fragrant essence of rosewater, which infuses every bite with an air of elegance and romance. The creamy coconut frosting adds a rich, tropical creaminess, while the raspberries provide a burst of freshness and tang.

Creating this cake is a labor of love. It begins with the careful blending of rosewater into the cake batter, followed by the layering of coconut frosting and a generous scattering of raspberries between each layer. The Rose, Coconut & Raspberry Cake is an invitation to savor the symphony of floral and fruity delights, a dessert that transforms any moment into a cherished memory.

- 25g water at 33°C
- 150g bubbly, lively second-build starter
- 200g Greek yogurt

- 175g sunflower oil
- 4 large free-range eggs, at room temperature
- 250g organic white flour (13% protein), plus extra for dusting
- 250g organic stoneground wholegrain flour (11.5% protein)
- 7g fine sea salt
- 140g dark soft brown sugar
- 1 teaspoon almond extract
- 8g dried edible rose petals
- unsalted butter, for greasing
- olive oil spray
- 300g fresh raspberries

To Finish:
- 25g toasted coconut flakes
- handful of fresh edible organic rose petals
- 1–2 tablespoons raspberry cordial

MIX:
1. In a large bowl, whisk together the water and sourdough starter. Gently mix in the yogurt, sunflower oil, eggs, flours, salt, sugar, almond extract and dried rose petals, stirring until all the are combined. Leave to stand for 30 minutes. Meanwhile, refresh the remaining starter in your jar and set aside.

PROVE:
2. Generously grease a 35cm tin with butter and dust with a little flour. Pour the batter into the prepared tin and spray the top with a little olive oil. Leave to prove on the kitchen table overnight.

BAKE:
3. Preheat your oven to 175°C/gas mark 3½. Stud 150g of the raspberries evenly into the top of the cake, then bake for 30–40 minutes. Remember every oven is different and baking times will vary a little, so keep an eye on your cake as it bakes. Test the cake for doneness by gently inserting a skewer into the centre – if it comes out clean, the cake is baked; if not, return it to the oven for another 3–4 minutes.
4. Remove from the oven. The raspberries in the cake with have mushed down a little during baking, so I like to push fresh raspberries into the top of the warm cake where the cooked fruit is.

Chapter 4

Classic Sourdough Breads

Gluten-Free Herb Pizza Crust

Prep time: 30 minutes | Cook time: 10 minutes | Makes 1 12-inch pizza crust

The Gluten-Free Herb Pizza Crust is a delicious and wholesome alternative to traditional pizza crusts, offering a symphony of flavors from fresh herbs and the versatility of being gluten-free. Picture a pizza crust infused with aromatic herbs, creating a fragrant canvas for your favorite toppings. This crust is a celebration of gluten-free baking with a savory twist.

At its core, this pizza crust is a delightful blend of gluten-free flours and a medley of fresh herbs like basil, oregano, and thyme. The result is a dough that's both tender and flavorful, providing a perfect foundation for your favorite pizza creations.

Pair this Gluten-Free Herb Pizza Crust with your choice of tomato sauce, cheese, and an array of toppings, from vegetables to meats or even seafood. The herbs in the crust add a layer of complexity that elevates your pizza to a gourmet experience.

Creating this crust is a straightforward process. The gluten-free flours are combined with herbs, and the dough is formed using standard pizza-making techniques. As it bakes, the herbs infuse the crust with their aromatic goodness, creating a tantalizing aroma and an unforgettable flavor profile.

The result is a Gluten-Free Herb Pizza Crust that's not just for those with dietary restrictions but a delicious option for anyone looking to enjoy a flavorful twist on classic pizza. Whether you're a seasoned gluten-free eater or simply a fan of gourmet pizza, this crust is sure to delight your taste buds with every slice.

- 356 g gluten-free all-purpose flour
- 8 g of dried basil
- 8 g of dried oregano
- 4 g of baking powder
- 2 g xanthan gum
- 4 g kosher salt
- 240 g of lukewarm water
- 28 g of olive oil
- 12 g of sugar
- 7.5 g of active dry yeast

1. Gather all the necessary ingredients and equipment.
2. In a medium-sized bowl, combine the gluten-free all-purpose flour, dried basil, dried oregano, baking powder, xanthan gum, and kosher salt. Mix well and set aside.
3. In another small bowl, mix together the active dry yeast, sugar, olive oil, and lukewarm water. Stir until everything is combined. You'll notice some lumps, but that's okay. Let this mixture sit for about 30 minutes at room temperature. During this time, it will become frothy, bubbly, and develop a strong yeast aroma.
4. Add the yeast mixture to the flour mixture and mix on low speed for about three to four minutes. The dough will become thick and sticky.
5. Allow the dough to rise in a warm place for 30 minutes, covering it with a lint-free towel or plastic wrap.
6. While the dough is rising, preheat your oven to 425 degrees Fahrenheit. Prepare a pizza pan by lightly greasing it and dusting it with gluten-free flour.
7. Once the dough has risen, use damp fingers to spread it onto the prepared pizza pan. Be sure to have a dish of water nearby to keep your fingertips moist as you work with the dough.

Chocolate Chip Sourdough Scones

Chocolate Chip Sourdough Scones are a delightful fusion of tangy sourdough and sweet chocolate chips,Imagine sinking your teeth into a warm, flaky scone studded with gooey chocolate chips—a flavor and texture experience that's nothing short of divine.

These scones showcase the magic of sourdough,The chocolate chips, with their melty sweetness, add a delightful contrast, making each bite an exquisite balance of flavors.

Pair these Chocolate Chip Sourdough Scones with a steaming cup of coffee or a tall glass of milk for a cozy morning indulgence, or enjoy them as a comforting afternoon snack.

Creating these scones is a joyful blend of baking tradition and sourdough artistry.Chocolate Chip Sourdough Scones are a testament to the creative possibilities of baking, offering a delicious twist on a beloved classic.

Dry:
- 250g all-purpose flour
- 100g granulated sugar
- 2.5g acceptable sea salt
- 10g baking powder
- 113g unsalted butter (frozen or very cold)
- 180g semi-sweet chocolate chips

Wet:
- 125g sourdough starter discard
- 1 large egg
- 10g vanilla extract
- 30g heavy cream (milk or half and half can be used)

Topping:
- 30g heavy cream (milk or half and half can be used)
- 45g sanding sugar (coarse sugar)

1. Sift the all-purpose flour, granulated sugar, sea salt, and baking powder into a suitable-sized bowl. Whisk to combine.
2. Grate the unsalted butter into the bowl with a cheese grater. Use a fork to toss the grated butter with the flour mixture, coating and separating the chunks of butter.
3. Use a pastry cutter or a bench scraper to chop the flour into the butter until the mixture resembles coarse crumbs the size of small peas. Mix the semi-sweet chocolate chips into the dry mixture.

Cranberry Pecan Bread

Prep time: 10 minutes | Cook time: 20 minutes | Makes 1 loaf

Cranberry Pecan Bread is a delightful celebration of flavors and textures, combining the tart zing of cranberries with the earthy richness of pecans. Imagine a and generously studded with crunchy pecans, each slice a harmonious blend of sweet, tangy, and nutty notes.

This bread captures the essence of the holiday season with the bright burst of cranberries, which provide a playful tartness. The pecans, with their toasty, buttery character, add depth and a satisfying crunch to every bite.

Pair this Cranberry Pecan Bread with a slather of creamy butter or a drizzle of honey for a simple yet indulgent treat. It's perfect for festive breakfasts, brunches, or as a delightful addition to a holiday bread basket.

Creating this bread is a labor of love that involves the art of baking and the joy of celebrating seasonal ingredients.Cranberries and pecans are generously folded into the mix, creating a bread that's as visually appealing as it is delicious.

- 200 g unbleached all-purpose flour
- 200 g whole wheat flour
- 20 g pecan pieces
- 20 g dried cranberries
- 10 g salt
- 200 g active starter
- 225 g water

1. In a medium mixing bowl, stir together the flours, pecan pieces, dried cranberries, and salt. As you continue the stretch and fold sessions, the pecans and cranberries will become evenly incorporated throughout. Cover the bowl and let the dough rise until about doubled, usually 4 to 8 hours or overnight.
2. Gently turn out the dough onto a floured work surface and shape it. Cover and let rise for about 4 hours or until nicely risen.
3. Slash the top. Preheat the oven to 400 to 450° and bake for 40 to 50 minutes or until done. Cool on a wire rack.

Rosemary Sourdough Bread

Prep time: 25 minutes | Cook time: 25 minutes | Serves 1

Rosemary Sourdough Bread is a fragrant and flavorful masterpiece that marries the earthy aroma of fresh rosemary with the tangy complexity of sourdough. Tantalizes your taste buds but also fills your kitchen with the inviting scent of Mediterranean herbs.

At its heart, this bread features the characteristic tanginess of sourdough, which results from the natural fermentation process. The addition of rosemary adds a layer of complexity, with its piney, citrusy notes that perfectly complement the mild acidity of the sourdough.

Pair this Rosemary Sourdough Bread with a drizzle of high-quality olive oil and a sprinkle of flaky sea salt for a simple yet luxurious appetizer. Alternatively, use it as a canvas for your favorite sandwiches or serve it alongside a bowl of hearty soup for a comforting meal.

Crafting this bread is a labor of love that involves the art of sourdough fermentation. Fresh rosemary is incorporated into the mix, infusing the dough with its aromatic essence. As the bread bakes, the rosemary releases its fragrant oils, creating a sensory experience that's as delightful as it is delicious.

- 60g rosemary leaves
- 65g olive oil
- 350g water
- 450g wheat flour
- 100g durum flour
- 40g rosemary oil (from above)
- 250g wheat sourdough starter
- 8g cane syrup
- 15g sea salt
- Optional: 20g semolina (for dusting on loaves)

1. In a dough mixer, combine all the bread ingredients except for the sea salt. Mix until the dough is elastic. When it's time to add the salt, do so at the end. If kneading by hand, stretch the dough and fold it over itself repeatedly until it's elastic.
2. Allow the dough to rise until it doubles in size.
3. Flour a work surface and sprinkle with semolina. If you have bannetons, use them for proofing. Alternatively, you can use kitchen towels as makeshift supports.
4. Let the loaves rise until they double in size, which should take around 60 to 90 minutes.
5. Preheat two oven plates to 480°F (250°C), one with a rack directly below it.

Simple Sourdough Focaccia

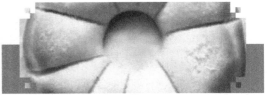

Prep time: 20 minutes | Cook time: 30 minutes | Serves 8-10

Simple Sourdough Focaccia is a delightful Italian classic that takes on a tangy twist, thanks to the magic of sourdough fermentation. land, perhaps, a few cherry tomatoes or olives—a bread that not only transports you to the heart of Italy but also celebrates the art of sourdough baking.

At its core, this focaccia boasts the distinctive tanginess of sourdough, which infuses each bite with a complexity of flavors. The olive oil adds a luscious richness, while the flaky sea salt provides a satisfying contrast of textures.

Enjoy this Simple Sourdough Focaccia as an appetizer, a snack, It's a versatile bread that pairs beautifully with dips, cheeses, and charcuterie.

Creating this focaccia is a rewarding culinary adventure that involves the art of sourdough fermentation.Once shaped and dimpled, the focaccia is generously drizzled with olive oil and adorned with your choice of toppings, such as herbs, tomatoes, or olives.

- 120 ml active sourdough starter
- 235 ml water
- 10 ml honey or agave nectar
- 120 ml olive oil (plus an additional 60 ml for drizzling)
- 530 ml all-purpose flour
- 7 ml salt
- toppings as desired

1. In a large bowl, mix together the starter, water, honey, and half of the olive oil.
2. Rest for 10 minutes, then use the "stretch and fold" method to develop the gluten. Repeat this process three times.
3. Cover the dough and let it sit overnight or until it has doubled in size.
4. In the morning, add the remaining 60 mL of olive oil to a baking pan. Fold your dough into a rectangular shape and place it in the baking pan.
5. Cover and let it rise for 2-3 hours.
6. Preheat the oven to 210°C (425°F). When the dough is finished rising for the second time, oil your fingers and press into it a few times, creating the classic dimpled look of focaccia bread.
7. At this point, you may choose to add any toppings or herbs you desire. Drizzle with olive oil, then bake for 25-30 minutes.

Sourdough Ciabatta Bread

Prep time: 20 minutes | Cook time: 20 minutes | Serves 4

Sourdough Ciabatta Bread is a rustic Italian classic that takes on a tangy twist, thanks to the magic of sourdough fermentation. Imagine a golden, artisanal loaf with a crisp, crackling crust and an airy, chewy crumb—an Italian bread that not only transports you to a Tuscan village but also celebrates the art of sourdough baking.

At the heart of this bread is the distinctive tanginess of sourdough, which provides depth and complexity to each bite. The open crumb structure and chewy texture are perfect for soaking up olive oil, balsamic vinegar, or savoring on its own.

Enjoy this Sourdough Ciabatta Bread as a side to complement a range of Italian dishes or slice it for sandwiches with your favorite fillings. It's a versatile bread that's equally delightful for dipping, toasting, or enjoying as a standalone treat.

Creating this bread is a labor of love, a journey that involves the art of sourdough fermentation and the mastery of rustic breadmaking. The dough is prepared with care, allowing it to rise and develop its characteristic tangy flavor and open crumb structure. Once shaped into the iconic ciabatta form, the bread is baked to perfection, resulting in a loaf that captures the rustic charm of Italian cuisine.

Each slice is a reminder of the joy of artisanal baking and the timeless allure of Mediterranean flavors. Sourdough Ciabatta Bread is an invitation to savor the essence of Italy in a bread that's as versatile as it is delicious, offering a perfect marriage of tradition and tangy twist.

- 355 ml water
- 10 ml salt
- 120 ml active sourdough starter
- 830 ml bread flour

1. Whisk the water and salt in a large bowl. Add the starter and stir. Next, add bread flour and stir until there is no more dry flour and loose dough forms.
2. Knead the ciabatta dough for 1-2 minutes until all of the flour is moistened. Cover the ciabatta dough with a clean kitchen towel and let it sit for 30 minutes.
3. Remove the towel from the ciabatta dough and wet your fingertips with water.
4. Grab the top portion of the dough, stretch it upward, and bring the dough over the center of the bowl.
5. Turn the bowl 90 degrees, then stretch the sourdough bread dough upward and bring it over the center of the bowl.
6. Let the ciabatta dough rest for 30 minutes, repeat steps 4 and 5 twice and let the dough rest for 30 minutes each time.
7. Repeat steps 4 and 5 for the final time and allow the dough to rest for 30 minutes.
8. Place the dough into a clean greased bowl with a lid, cover it and let it rest for 3-4 hours until it doubles in volume.
9. Place the ciabatta into the fridge and let it chill overnight. Then, remove the ciabatta from the refrigerator, remove the lid, and sprinkle it generously with flour.
10. Invert the ciabatta dough onto a floured surface and press it into a rectangular shape. Slice the ciabatta dough into two vertically and divide each half in half to create 4 loaves.

Sourdough Cornbread

Prep time: 20 minutes | Cook time: 30-40 minutes | Serves 8-10

Sourdough Cornbread is a delightful twist on a beloved Southern classic, infusing the comfort of cornbread with the tangy charm of sourdough. Imagine a golden, crumbly wedge of cornbread with a slight tanginess that elevates this Southern staple to new heights—a bread that not only warms your heart but also celebrates the art of sourdough baking.

At its core, this cornbread boasts the distinctive tanginess of sourdough, which adds depth and complexity to each bite. The cornmeal provides a satisfying texture and a sweet, nutty flavor that perfectly complements the sourdough tang.

Enjoy this Sourdough Cornbread as a side to accompany hearty stews, barbecue, or a traditional Southern meal. It's a versatile bread that pairs beautifully with butter, honey, or even a dollop of tangy barbecue sauce.

The result is Sourdough Cornbread that not only captures the essence of Southern hospitality but also embodies the simple joy of savoring tradition with a tangy twist.Sourdough Cornbread is an invitation to savor the best of both worlds—Southern comfort and sourdough sophistication.

- 120 mL active sourdough starter
- 355 mL all-purpose flour
- 355 mL cornmeal
- 3 mL salt
- 5 mL baking powder
- 3 mL baking soda
- 120 mL sugar
- 120 mL honey or agave nectar
- 3 large eggs
- 295 mL buttermilk
- 180 mL butter, melted

1. Preheat the oven to 205°C (400°F).
2. Combine the dry ingredients in one bowl.
3. In a separate bowl, combine the wet ingredients.
4. Slowly add the dry mixture to the wet mixture, stirring until just combined.
5. Pour the batter into a 9-inch greased or buttered baking pan.
6. Bake for 30-40 minutes or until a toothpick inserted in the center comes out clean.

Ciabattas

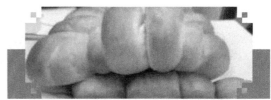

Prep time: 12-16 hours | Cook time: 20 minutes | Makes 1 loaf

Ciabattas are a classic Italian bread known for their rustic appearance, chewy texture, and crusty exterior. Making sandwiches, or tearing apart for dipping in sauces.

These iconic Italian loaves are characterized by their slightly tangy flavor, which develops from the natural fermentation of a preferment or biga.

Each slice of Ciabatta is a reminder of the rustic charm of Italian cuisine and the simple joy of savoring a beloved classic. Ciabattas are a testament to the artistry of breadmaking and the timeless appeal of Italian flavors.

For Activating the Starter:
- 269 grams (1 cup) sourdough starter
- 113 grams (½ cup) lukewarm (32°C to 38°C) pure filtered or bottled water
- 113 grams (1 cup) whole-wheat flour

For the Bread Dough:
- 340 grams (1¼ cups) active sourdough starter
- 5 grams (1 teaspoon) instant dry yeast
- 184 grams (1½ cups) unbleached bread flour, plus more for dusting
- 17 grams (1 tablespoon) fine sea salt
- 5 grams (1 teaspoon) sugar
- 57 grams (¼ cup) lukewarm (32°C to 38°C) milk
- Cornmeal or semolina flour, for dusting

1. Combine the starter, lukewarm water, plus flour, completely incorporating the fixings into the starter, at least 6 to 12 hours before making the dough, in a medium bowl. Wrap, then let sit on your counter until ready to use.
2. The next day, in the bowl of a stand mixer fitted with the dough hook, or a large bowl. Increase the speed to number two and mix for 6 minutes until all the ingredients are well incorporated, or stir by hand.
3. Generously coat a large bowl with olive oil and transfer the dough to it, turning to coat all sides. Wrap the bowl using a clean kitchen towel and place the bowl in the oven, light on, rise for 1 to 2 hours, or until the dough doubles in size.
4. Flour a breadboard or clean work surface and turn the dough out onto it. Stretch the dough into a rectangle. Re-cover the dough and let rise for 1 hour.
5. Sprinkle a baking sheet with cornmeal and place the ciabatta loaf on it.Re-cover the dough and let rise 1 hour more in a warm, draft-free place.

Sun-Dried Tomato and Basil Bread

Prep time: 10 minutes | Cook time: 20 minutes | Makes 1 loaf

Sun-Dried Tomato and Basil Bread is a culinary masterpiece that transports your taste buds straight to the sun-soaked hills of the Mediterranean. Imagine a golden, rustic loaf infused with the bold, sweet intensity of sun-dried tomatoes and the aromatic charm of fresh basil—a bread that not only tantalizes your senses but also embodies the essence of Mediterranean cuisine.

This bread is a delightful blend of flavors and textures. The sun-dried tomatoes add a burst of sweet and tangy richness, while the basil infuses each bite with a fragrant herbal note. The combination is a harmonious symphony of Mediterranean ingredients that's perfect for savoring the tastes of summer all year round.

Pair this Sun-Dried Tomato and Basil Bread with a drizzle of extra-virgin olive oil, a spread of creamy goat cheese, or as an accompaniment to your favorite Mediterranean-inspired dishes. It's a versatile bread that complements everything from salads to antipasto platters or makes a fantastic base for gourmet sandwiches.

Creating this bread is a culinary journey that involves the artistry of breadmaking and the celebration of Mediterranean flavors.

The result is a Sun-Dried Tomato and Basil Bread that embodies the spirit of the Mediterranean, offering a delightful explosion of flavors and a sensory experience that transports you to a sun-drenched seaside cafe with every bite. Each slice is a reminder of the magic of Mediterranean cuisine and the simple joy of savoring the essence of the region in a single, delicious loaf.

- 225 g water
- 200 g active starter
- 200 g unbleached all-purpose flour
- 200 g whole wheat flour
- 10 g salt
- 30 g sun-dried tomatoes, chopped into small pieces (no bigger than a chocolate chip)
- 1 heaping tsp. dried basil leaves (do not use ground basil)

1. In a large bowl, mix all the ingredients except the sun-dried tomatoes and basil. Let the dough sit for about 30 minutes. Keeping the dough in the container, stretch and fold the dough, cover the bowl, and let it rest for 30 minutes; stretch and fold the dough a second time, cover the bowl, and let it rest for another 30 minutes.
2. Now add the sun-dried tomatoes and basil, doing your best to sprinkle the pieces throughout the dough; stretch and fold the dough 4 more times, covering the bowl and letting the dough rest 30 minutes between each time. With each subsequent stretch and fold session, you'll notice that the sun-dried tomatoes and basil will become more evenly distributed throughout the dough.
3. Cover the bowl and let the dough rise until about doubled, usually 4 to 8 hours or overnight.
4. Gently turn out the dough onto a floured work surface and shape it. Cover and let rise for about 4 hours or until about doubled.
5. Slash the top. Preheat the oven to 400 to 450° and bake for 40 to 45 minutes or until done. Cool on a wire rack.

Garlic Butter Couronne

Prep time: 10 minutes | Cook time: 40 minutes | Makes 1 loaf

The Garlic Butter Couronne is a heavenly creation that marries the rich, savory goodness of garlic butter with the delicate flakiness of a crown-shaped pastry. Imagine a golden-brown, spiral-shaped bread adorned with layers of fragrant garlic butter, each bite a savory explosion of flavor and texture.

This pastry features the indulgent combination of garlic and butter, resulting in a luscious filling that's both aromatic and rich. The couronne's layers of flaky dough and garlic-infused butter create a delightful contrast of crispy and tender textures.

Pair this Garlic Butter Couronne with a bowl of soup for a comforting meal or serve it as an elegant appetizer at gatherings. It's a versatile pastry that adds a touch of culinary sophistication to any occasion.

Creating this couronne is an artful process that involves the layering and shaping of dough with generous amounts of garlic butter. The aroma of garlic permeates your kitchen, making each slice of this couronne a delectable testament to the magic of garlic butter.

Dough:

- 1 large egg
- 160 g (¾ cup) whole milk
- 35 g (2½ tbsp) extra-virgin olive oil
- 150 g (⅔ cup) active sourdough starter
- 325 g (2⅔ cups) bread flour
- 60 g (½ cup) whole wheat flour
- 28 g (2 tbsp) granulated sugar
- 7 g (1 tsp) salt

Garlic Butter:

- 6 cloves garlic, crushed
- 10 g (¾ cup) chopped parsley leaves
- 57 g (4 tbsp) unsalted butter, softened
- 15 g (1 tbsp) extra-virgin olive oil
- 28 g (2 tbsp) unsalted butter, melted

Day 1:

1. In a large bowl, whisk together the egg, milk, olive oil and active starter until they're fully combined. Stir in the bread flour, whole wheat flour, sugar and salt, and continue mixing until all the flour has been hydrated.
2. Turn the dough out onto a lightly floured work surface and knead about 10 minutes, until the dough looks smooth. Cover the bowl with plastic wrap and set it aside at room temperature to rise for 4 to 6 hours, or until the dough has doubled in size.
3. Deflate it by pushing down on it, then round it into a tight ball and place it in an airtight container in the refrigerator for an overnight rest.

Day 2:

1. To make the garlic butter, combine the garlic, parsley, softened butter and olive oil in a small bowl and set aside.
2. Line a 23-cm round cake pan with parchment paper.
3. On a lightly floured work surface, using a rolling pin, roll the dough out into a 23 x 45–cm rectangle with the long edge facing you. Spread the garlic butter evenly over the dough. Twist the two pieces of dough around each other and join the ends together to form a circular crown. Pinch the ends to hold them together.
4. Transfer your couronne to the lined cake pan. Place the pan in a clean plastic bag and leave to proof at room temperature until the dough has doubled, 2 to 4 hours.
5. Preheat the oven to 175°C.

Chapter 5

Whole Grain Breads and Sandwich Breads

Wheat and Almond Focaccia

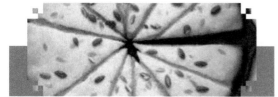

Prep time: 2 hours | Cook time: 40 minutes | Makes 2 focaccia

Wheat and Almond Focaccia is a delightful variation of the classic Italian bread, infusing the rustic charm of wheat flour with the rich nuttiness of almonds. Imagine a golden, dimpled flatbread adorned with toasted almond slices and a drizzle of olive oil, each bite offering a balance of nutty goodness and the comforting familiarity of focaccia.

At its core, this focaccia boasts the signature chewiness and dimpled surface of the classic Italian bread, with the added dimension of almond flavor and crunch. The almond slices provide a delightful contrast to the tender crumb and the olive oil infuses each bite with a hint of Mediterranean richness.

Enjoy Wheat and Almond Focaccia as an appetizer, a side to complement Italian dishes, or even as a base for gourmet sandwiches. It's a versatile bread that pairs beautifully with dips, cheeses, and charcuterie.

The result is a Wheat and Almond Focaccia that Each bite is a reminder of the magic of breadmaking and the joy of savoring the perfect marriage of wheat and almonds in a single, delightful loaf.

- 120 g wheat flour
- 120 g almond flour
- 2.5 g salt
- 2.5 g cayenne pepper
- 120 ml olive oil
- 2 garlic cloves, minced
- 15 ml baking powder
- 5 eggs, whisked
- 15 ml dried rosemary
- Cooking spray

1. In a bowl, mix the wheat flour with the almond flour, salt, cayenne pepper, minced garlic, baking powder, and dried rosemary. Stir well to combine.
2. Gradually add the olive oil to the dry ingredients while stirring continuously until everything is well mixed.
3. Pour the batter into two square pans that have been greased with cooking spray.
4. Bake at 165°C (330°F) for about 40 minutes or until the top is golden brown and a toothpick inserted into the center comes out clean.
5. Allow the baked bread to cool down before slicing and serving.

Avocado Whole Wheat Bread

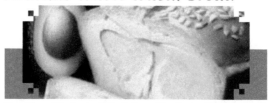

Prep time: 10 minutes | Cook time: 40 minutes | Makes 1 loaf

Avocado Whole Wheat Bread is a delightful fusion of the creamy richness. Imagine a loaf of bread with a tender crumb and a subtle avocado flavor, each slice embodying the earthy richness of whole wheat and the smooth creaminess of avocados—a bread that not only satisfies your hunger but also celebrates the nutritious allure of avocados.

At its core, this bread features the healthful benefits of whole wheat flour, which provides a hearty, nutty flavor and a wholesome texture. The avocado adds a touch of creaminess and subtle green notes, resulting in a bread that's both nutritious and delicious.

Enjoy Avocado Whole Wheat Bread as a versatile and nutritious option for sandwiches, toast, or a hearty side to complement a variety of dishes. It's a bread that pairs beautifully with fresh greens, tomatoes, and your choice of protein for a wholesome sandwich.

The result is Avocado Whole Wheat Bread that captures the essence of wholesome goodness. Each slice is a reminder of the simple joy of savoring the fusion of health and flavor in a single, green-infused loaf.

- 120 g whole wheat flour
- 5 g baking powder
- 2.5 g cinnamon powder
- 100 g sugar
- 1 egg, whisked
- 60 g butter, melted
- 2.5 ml vanilla extract
- 5 ml lemon juice
- 240 g avocado, peeled, pitted, and mashed

1. In a bowl, mix the whole wheat flour with baking powder and cinnamon powder. Add the sugar and stir well until all the dry ingredients are combined.
2. In a separate bowl, whisk the egg, then add melted butter, vanilla extract, and lemon juice. Mix until well combined.
3. Add the mashed avocado to the wet mixture and stir until it's evenly incorporated.
4. Combine the wet and dry mixtures, stirring until you obtain a smooth dough.
5. Knead the dough for about 10 minutes, then transfer it to a loaf pan.
6. Bake the bread at 160°C (320°F) for approximately 40 minutes, or until it's cooked through, and a toothpick inserted into the center comes out clean.

Eric's Whole Grain Waffles

Prep time: 30 minutes | Cooking time: 4 minutes | Serves 4

Eric's Whole Grain Waffles are a delightful morning indulgence that marries the hearty goodness of whole grains with the comforting warmth of waffles. Imagine a plate stacked high with waffles, each one boasting a crispy exterior and a tender, whole grain interior—a breakfast treat that not only fills your belly but also nourishes your body with the wholesome goodness of grains.

At the heart of these waffles is the blend of whole grains, which may include options like whole wheat, oats, or even quinoa flour. This medley of grains provides a nutty, earthy flavor and a hearty texture that's both comforting and satisfying.

Creating these waffles is a labor of love, blending the art of baking with the science of whole grains. Once cooked to golden perfection in a waffle iron, they emerge with a satisfying aroma that fills your kitchen and beckons you to the breakfast table.

The result is Eric's Whole Grain Waffles that capture the essence of hearty breakfast comfort and the joy of savoring the natural goodness of whole grains. Each bite is a reminder of the simple pleasure of a homemade breakfast and the nourishing power of grains in every delicious mouthful.

- 300 grams water
- 300 grams milk
- 300 grams whole-grain einkorn flour
- 100 grams sourdough discard
- 3 grams salt (½ teaspoon)
- 3 grams baking soda (½ teaspoon)
- 2 eggs (optional)
- Oil or butter, for greasing

1. In a medium bowl with space for tripling, mix the water, milk, flour, and sourdough discard. Cover and let sit at room temperature overnight.
2. Preheat your waffle iron.
3. Whisk the salt, baking soda, and eggs (if using) into the batter.
4. Spray oil or brush butter on the waffle iron. Scoop ⅓ cup of batter onto the waffle iron and cook according to your waffle-iron maker's instructions for 3 to 4 minutes. Repeat for the remaining batter.

Cranberry Walnut

Prep time: 60 minutes | Cooking time: 50 minutes | Serves 1

Cranberry Walnut Muffins are a delightful fusion of tart cranberries and earthy walnuts, combining to create a morning treat that's both nutty and tangy. harmonious blend of sweet and tart flavors, as well as a satisfying crunch.

At the heart of these muffins is the contrast between the tartness of cranberries and the earthy richness of walnuts. The walnuts add a depth and satisfying texture that elevates these muffins to a new level of deliciousness.

Pair Cranberry Walnut Muffins with a hot cup of coffee or a glass of freshly squeezed orange juice for a delightful breakfast or a mid-morning snack. They're a versatile treat that suits a variety of occasions and tastes.

The result is Cranberry Walnut Muffins that capture the essence of seasonal baking and the joy of savoring Each muffin is a reminder of the simple pleasure of a homemade treat and the natural beauty of these complementary ingredients.

- 250 grams all-purpose or bread flour
- 250 grams whole grain flour
- 400 grams water
- 70 grams sourdough starter
- 10 grams salt (1¾ teaspoons)
- 140 grams dried cranberries
- 100 grams walnuts (toasting is optional; see step 1)

1. If you want to toast your walnuts, spread them on a baking sheet and bake them in a preheated oven at 175°C (350°F) for 5 to 10 minutes. Let them cool for about 10 minutes before you mix them into the dough.
2. Thoroughly mix the flours, water, starter, and salt in a medium bowl.
3. Add the cranberries and walnuts and continue mixing until they're evenly distributed. Note the level of the dough and the time. Cover the dough and let it rest on your counter for 30 minutes.
4. with damp fingertips, stretch and fold the dough, lifting the edge of one side of the dough and folding it over to the other side. Cover and let the dough rest again for 30 minutes.
5. Perform three more rounds of stretching and folding as in step 4, separated by 30-minute rests.
6. When the dough has grown by about 50% and the surface is puffy, end the bulk fermentation. Depending mostly on temperature, this will likely be 6 to 10 hours from mixing.

Soft Sandwich Bread

Prep time: 10 minutes | Cook time: 20 minutes | Makes 1 loaf

Soft Sandwich Bread is the epitome of comfort and versatility in the world of bread. Imagine slices of this bread, pillowy and tender, with a subtle hint of sweetness—a bread that not only cradles your favorite sandwich fillings but also has a delightful melt-in-your-mouth quality.

At its core, this bread is the embodiment of simplicity and nostalgia. Its softness makes it perfect for sandwiches of all kinds, from classic PB&Js to gourmet deli creations. The subtle sweetness enhances the overall experience without overwhelming the flavors of your chosen fillings.

Whether you're making a hearty club sandwich or a delicate cucumber tea sandwich, Soft Sandwich Bread is the canvas that elevates your sandwich creations.

Creating this bread is a culinary journey that involves precision in mixing, kneading, and rising. The dough is allowed to rest and develop its characteristic softness and structure. Baking it to perfection results in loaves that fill your kitchen with the irresistible aroma of freshly baked bread.

The result is Soft Sandwich Bread that captures the essence of homemade comfort and the simple joy of crafting delicious sandwiches from scratch. Each slice is a reminder of the heartwarming pleasure of a well-made sandwich, where the bread is as important as the fillings it holds.

- 28 g butter
- 240 g milk, heated almost to boiling
- 224 g active starter
- 12 g granulated sugar
- 9 g salt
- 350 g unbleached all-purpose flour
- 1 egg, beaten

1. Place the butter in the hot milk and stir to melt the butter; cool the milk mixture to 100°.
2. In a large mixing bowl, stir together the milk mixture, starter, sugar, and salt to combine. Add the flour a bit at a time until you can no longer mix the dough by hand. Turn out the dough onto a floured work surface and knead in the remaining flour. Continue kneading for several minutes, using as little extra flour as possible. The dough should be soft and slightly sticky.
3. Shape the dough into a round, smooth ball and place it in a large oiled or greased bowl, turning the dough to coat all surfaces. Cover the bowl with plastic wrap and allow it to rest at room temperature for 30 minutes.
4. Stretch and fold the dough a total of 2 times at 30-minute intervals and keeping the bowl covered between times. Let the covered dough rest at room temperature for 1 hour; then stretch and fold 3 times at 1-hour intervals, keeping the bowl covered between times.
5. By now, the dough should be very lively and light, but if not, cover the dough and let it rest for an hour or two longer.

Garlic Sandwich Bread

Prep time: 2 hours | Cook time: 40 minutes | Makes 1 loaf

Garlic Sandwich Bread is a delectable fusion of the savory richness of garlic and the comfort of a classic sandwich loaf. Imagine slices of this bread, each one boasting a soft, tender crumb infused with the aromatic essence of garlic—a bread that not only cradles your favorite sandwich fillings but also imparts a delightful garlic flavor to elevate your sandwich game.

At its core, this bread features the bold and savory notes of garlic, which add depth and complexity to each bite. The garlic's aroma and flavor permeate the tender crumb, offering a sensory experience that's as irresistible as it is delicious.

Pair Garlic Sandwich Bread with a variety of fillings, from roasted vegetables to deli meats and cheeses, to create gourmet sandwiches that burst with flavor. It's also perfect for crafting garlic bread to accompany your favorite pasta dishes or serving as a side to hearty soups.

Creating this bread is a culinary adventure that combines the art of baking with the aromatic allure of garlic.Baking it to perfection results in loaves that fill your kitchen with the irresistible scent of homemade comfort food.

The result is Garlic Sandwich Bread that captures the essence of savory indulgence and the joy of savoring the bold, aromatic flavors of garlic in every bite. Each slice is a reminder of the magic of garlic in enhancing the flavor of your favorite sandwiches and the comfort of homemade bread that elevates every meal.

- 240 ml hot water
- 30 g sugar
- 10 g dry yeast
- 60 ml avocado oil
- 3 garlic cloves, minced
- 480 g coconut flour
- 2.5 g ground coriander
- 2.5 g dried rosemary
- 30 g butter, melted
- 2.5 g turmeric powder

1. In a large bowl, mix the coconut flour with minced garlic, ground coriander, dried rosemary, and the other dry ingredients. Stir well until all the dry ingredients are combined.
2. In a separate bowl, combine hot water and sugar, then sprinkle the dry yeast on top. Allow it to sit for a few minutes until it becomes foamy.
3. Add avocado oil to the yeast mixture and mix well.
4. Gradually add the wet mixture to the dry mixture, kneading the dough for about 10 minutes until it's smooth and well combined.
5. Cover the dough and leave it to rise for 1 hour and 30 minutes in a warm place, or until it has doubled in size.
6. After the first rise, transfer the dough to a loaf pan and let it rise for an additional 30 minutes.
7. Preheat your oven to 190°C (370°F).
8. Bake the bread for approximately 40 minutes or until it's cooked through and has a golden crust.
9. Remove the bread from the oven, brush the top with melted butter and turmeric powder mixture for added flavor and color.
10. Allow the bread to cool, then slice and serve.

Spiced Cheese Sandwich Crackers

Prep time: 10 minutes | Cook time: 32 minutes | Serves 4

Spiced Cheese Sandwich Crackers are a delectable fusion of savory cheese, aromatic spices, and the satisfying crunch of crackers. Picture bite-sized crackers, sandwiching a zesty cheese filling, with a hint of warmth and spice that dances on your taste buds—a snack that's not only addictive but also offers a delightful balance of flavors and textures.

At the heart of these crackers is the combination of creamy cheese and a medley of spices, which may include paprika, cayenne pepper, or even a touch of garlic. The result is a bold, savory filling that's perfectly complemented by the crispness of the crackers.

Creating these crackers is a culinary adventure that involves the art of mixing, rolling, and cutting. The cheese filling is crafted with care, ensuring it's perfectly seasoned with the chosen spices. The cracker dough is rolled thin and carefully assembled with the filling, resulting in bite-sized sandwich crackers that offer a satisfying crunch and an explosion of flavor.

The result is Spiced Cheese Sandwich Crackers that capture the essence of savory snacking with a spicy twist. Each bite is a reminder of the joy of indulging in a satisfyingly crunchy and boldly seasoned snack that elevates your snacking experience to a new level of deliciousness.

- 200 g (1 cup) starter (fed, unfed or discard)
- 100 g (scant 1 cup) rolled oats
- 100 g (scant 1 cup) whole wheat flour, plus more for dusting
- 80 g (½ cup) seed mix (see Top Tip)
- 50 g (¼ cup) water
- 60 g (4 tbsp) olive oil
- 30 g (3 tsp) runny honey or pure maple syrup
- 14 g (2 tbsp) spice mix of your choice (I use a chip seasoning mix)
- 7 g (1 tsp) salt, or to taste

Sandwich Filling:

200 g (7 oz) hard cheese, in 1 to 2 mm-thick slices (choose a cheese that melts without completely disintegrating; I use Cheddar, Red Leicester or a Mexican spiced cheese)

1. In a medium-sized mixing bowl, mix together all the ingredients except the cheese to form a stiff dough. Ensure that the ingredients are well and evenly combined. Cover the bowl with a clean shower cap or your choice of cover and leave it on the counter overnight. The dough will grow and puff up slightly overnight, but it will not have a huge rise and does not need to.
2. When you are ready to bake, decide whether you would like to bake in a preheated oven or from a cold start. If preheating, set the oven to 200°C convection or 220°C conventional.
3. Dust your kitchen counter with a little flour, turn the dough out onto the counter and use a rolling pin to roll the dough out to a 60 x 30–cm rectangle. Place the cheese slices on one of the rectangles, covering the entire area. Lift the other half of the dough and place it on top of the cheese.
4. Using a pizza cutter or sharp knife, cut the dough into 1½-inch (4-cm) squares. If you would like larger crackers, cut the dough into bigger squares. Place the crackers on the prepared baking pan. They can be placed close as they do not spread sideways as they bake.

Chapter 6

Pan Loaves

The Easiest No-Knead Bread

Prep time: 3 hours 10 minutes | Cook time: 30 minutes | Makes 4-5 loaves

The Easiest No-Knead Bread is a testament to the simplicity and joy of homemade bread baking. Imagine a rustic, golden loaf with a crisp, crackling crust and an airy, tender crumb—a bread that not only fills your kitchen with the irresistible scent of freshly baked bread but also requires minimal effort and expertise.

At its core, this no-knead bread relies on the magic of time and fermentation. The result is a homemade bread that rivals artisanal loaves, without the need for intensive kneading.

Enjoy the Easiest No-Knead Bread as a versatile staple for sandwiches, toast, or a hearty side to complement a variety of dishes. It's a bread that pairs beautifully with butter, cheese, or your favorite dips and spreads.

The result is the Easiest No-Knead Bread that captures the essence of homemade comfort. Crafting your own bread with minimal effort—a true delight for the senses and a testament to the timeless allure of homemade bread.

- 710 g of lukewarm water
- 21 g of granulated yeast (equivalent to about 2 packets of any brand/style)
- 22 g of coarse salt
- 845 g of unbleached all-purpose flour

1. In a large mixing bowl, combine the lukewarm water (around 43°C), yeast, and salt. There's no need to wait for the yeast to dissolve; simply pour it into the water.
2. Add the unbleached all-purpose flour to the water mixture. You don't need to sift the flour; just measure it and add it to the bowl.
3. Stir the mixture with a wooden spoon or your hands until all the ingredients are evenly moistened. No kneading is required; just ensure the mixture is well combined.
4. Cover the bowl and place it in a warm spot to let the dough rise. It should roughly double in size. This typically takes about 2 hours.
5. Once the dough has risen, you can take a portion of it, about the size of a grapefruit, using floured hands. Avoid kneading the dough; simply shape it quickly into a ball. You can let it rest in the fridge for a few hours if you like, but if you're eager to bake, you can proceed immediately.

Sourdough Zeppoles

Prep time: 5 minutes | Cook time: 15 minutes | Makes about 3 dozen

Sourdough Zeppoles are a delightful fusion of Italian culinary tradition and the tangy charm of sourdough fermentation. Imagine bite-sized rounds of golden, fried dough, generously dusted with powdered sugar—a sweet treat that not only transports you to the streets of Italy but also celebrates the art of sourdough baking.

Sourdough Zeppoles are a delightful addition to any dessert table, whether you're celebrating a special occasion or simply indulging in a sweet moment. They're perfect for dipping into chocolate sauce, fruit compote, or enjoying with a cup of espresso.

The result is Sourdough Zeppoles that capture the essence of Italian dessert culture and the unique twist of sourdough. Each bite is a reminder of the joy of indulging in sweet, fried treats and the timeless allure of both Italian and sourdough flavors—a delightful marriage of tradition and tangy sophistication.

- 2 large eggs, at room temperature
- 125 g whole milk ricotta, at room temperature
- 120 g leftover starter
- ½ tsp pure vanilla extract
- 120 g all-purpose flour
- 10 g baking powder
- 50 g sugar
- pinch of fine sea salt
- 1.4 l vegetable oil, for frying
- powdered sugar, to serve

1. Whisk the eggs, ricotta, leftover starter, and vanilla extract in a large bowl. Add the flour, baking powder, sugar, and salt. Mix with a wooden spoon until just incorporated. The batter will be thick.
2. Pour the oil into an 20-cm pot. Warm over medium-high heat until it reaches about 182 to 185°C. If it floats to the top and is surrounded by small bubbles, it's ready. If not, allow the oil to come to temperature and try again.
3. Using a level tablespoon or mini ice cream scoop, gently lower a few spoonfuls of batter into the hot oil. Fry for about 3 to 4 minutes, turning occasionally, until puffed,Transfer to a paper towel-lined plate with a large slotted spoon. Adjust the heat if necessary, then finish frying the rest of the batter.

Cinnamon Raisin Light Wheat Pan Bread

Prep time: 10-16 hours | Cook time: 50 minutes | Makes 1 loaf

Cinnamon Raisin Light Wheat Pan Bread is a delightful blend of wholesome wheat, aromatic cinnamon, and plump raisins, creating a bread that's both nutritious and sweetly satisfying. Imagine slices of this golden loaf, each one infused with the comforting aroma of cinnamon and studded with juicy raisins—a bread that not only nourishes your body but also warms your heart with every bite.

At its core, this pan bread is a celebration of whole wheat flour, which provides a hearty, nutty flavor and a nutritious base. The cinnamon adds a warm, comforting spice, and the raisins bring a burst of natural sweetness to each slice. The result is a bread that's both wholesome and indulgent, perfect for breakfast, snack time, or dessert.

Enjoy Cinnamon Raisin Light Wheat Pan Bread toasted and slathered with butter or cream cheese for a cozy breakfast or afternoon treat. Its sweet and cinnamon-infused aroma will fill your kitchen, inviting you to savor the simple pleasures of homemade comfort food.

Creating this pan bread is a culinary journey that combines the art of baking with the richness of cinnamon and raisins. The dough is prepared with care, allowing it to rise and develop its characteristic flavor and texture. Once baked to a golden perfection, the loaf emerges with a slightly crisp crust and a tender crumb, ready to be sliced and savored.

The result is Cinnamon Raisin Light Wheat Pan Bread that captures the essence of nutritious comfort and the simple joy of savoring a slice that's both wholesome and sweet. Each bite is a reminder of the magic of combining the goodness of whole wheat, the warmth of cinnamon, and the natural sweetness of raisins in a single, comforting loaf.

- 350 grams all-purpose or bread flour
- 170 grams whole grain flour
- 340 grams water
- 150 grams sourdough starter
- 30 grams honey (1½ tablespoons)
- 12 grams salt (2 teaspoons)
- grams cinnamon (2 teaspoons)
- 120 grams raisins
- cooking oil for greasing

1. Thoroughly mix the bread flour, whole wheat flour, water, sourdough starter, honey, salt, and cinnamon in a medium bowl. Add the raisins and continue mixing until they're evenly distributed. Wrap and let the dough rest for 15 minutes, then give it a round of stretching and folding:
2. with your damp fingertips, stretch, then fold the dough, lifting the edge of one side of the dough and folding it over to the other side. Do two or three times, stretching and folding each side until it feels tighter.
3. Let the dough bulk ferment for 6 to 10 hours at room temperature, or until it has just about doubled in size.
4. Flour your countertop, scrape your dough out onto it, and shape it into a tube. While your dough rests on its seam, oil your loaf pan, then put the dough in the pan seam-side down.
5. Wrap and proof the dough within 2 to 4 hours. It is ready to bake when it has doubled in size or its highest part crests over the lip of a 23x13x7 cm loaf pan.

Sourdough Pita Bread

Prep time: 30 minutes | Cook time: 20 minutes | Serves 8

Sourdough Pita Bread is a delightful fusion of the tangy allure of sourdough and the versatile, pocketed nature of traditional pita. Mediterranean-inspired ingredients—a bread that not only adds a tangy twist to your dishes but also captures the heart of Mediterranean cuisine.

At its core, these pitas boast the distinctive tanginess of sourdough, which adds depth and complexity to each bite. The dough is prepared with care, allowing the sourdough starter to work its magic, creating a texture that's both tender and slightly chewy.

Sourdough Pita Bread is the perfect vehicle for creating mouthwatering sandwiches, wraps, or dipping into hummus and other Mediterranean dips. Its unique texture and tangy flavor make it an ideal partner for a variety of fillings and spreads.

The result is Sourdough Pita Bread that captures the essence of Mediterranean flavors and the tangy sophistication of sourdough.Pocketed morsel—a delightful marriage of tradition and modern culinary innovation.

- 227 g active sourdough starter
- 227 g of warm water
- 391 g of bread flour
- 28 g of olive oil
- 14 g of granulated sugar
- 7.5 g table salt

1. Feed Your Starter: Before starting, make sure your sourdough starter is active and has been recently fed.
2. Morning Mix: In the morning, combine the active sourdough starter, bread flour, 250g of softened unsalted butter, 3 large eggs, honey, and 7.5g of salt in a mixing bowl. This may take around 10 to 15 minutes in a stand mixer, or longer if you're kneading by hand. Avoid adding extra flour; the dough should be moist.
3. First Rise: Cover the dough tightly with plastic wrap, a damp cloth, or a tight-fitting lid, and place it in a warm location for 6-8 hours or until it has doubled in size.
4. Chill the Dough: Refrigerate the dough for a few hours or overnight. This helps the dough become firm and easier to shape.
5. Divide and Shape: Split the dough into two equal portions using a bench scraper. Cut each portion into 8 pieces, shaping them into tight balls.
6. Loaf Pans: Place eight dough balls into each loaf pan lined with parchment paper.

Oil-Free Focaccia

Prep time: 10 minutes | Cook time: 50 minutes | Serves 4

Oil-Free Focaccia is a delicious and wholesome take on the classic Italian bread that doesn't compromise on flavor or texture. Imagine a golden, herb-infused flatbread with a tender crumb and a slightly crisp crust—a bread that not only satisfies your cravings but also caters to a healthier lifestyle.

At its core, this focaccia showcases the simplicity of breadmaking with a healthier twist. It omits traditional olive oil, relying on clever alternatives like applesauce or mashed potatoes to maintain moisture and tenderness. The result is a bread that's lighter in fat but still rich in flavor.

Creating this bread is a culinary adventure that involves creative substitutions and a mindful approach to ingredients. Baking it to a golden perfection results in a focaccia that captures the essence of traditional Italian breadmaking with a modern, health-conscious twist.

Each bite of Oil-Free Focaccia is a reminder of the magic of wholesome ingredients and the satisfaction of savoring a lighter, yet still delicious, version of a classic favorite. It's a bread that embraces a mindful approach to cooking while preserving the essence of Italian cuisine—a true culinary delight for those seeking a healthier, but equally flavorful, alternative.

- 30 g (⅛ cup) active starter
- 250 g (1 cup) water
- 300 g (2½ cups) strong white bread flour
- 4 g (½ tsp) salt, or to taste

1. In the early evening, in a large mixing bowl, roughly mix together all the ingredients, until you have a shaggy, rough dough. Cover the bowl with a clean shower cap or your choice of cover and leave the bowl on the counter for 2 hours.
2. After the 2-hour rest, perform the first set of pulls and folds on the dough until it feels less sticky and comes together into a soft ball. It will be soft, sticky and stretchy and the ball of dough will not hold its shape. Cover the bowl again and leave it on your counter.
3. After another 1 to 2 hours, do another set of pulls and folds on the dough, covering the dough again once completed.
4. Leave the covered bowl on the counter overnight, typically 8 to 10 hours, at 18 to 20°C.

Manchego Spelt Crackers

Prep time: 10 minutes | Cook time: 40 minutes | Makes 45 crackers

Manchego Spelt Crackers are a delightful fusion of the nutty charm of spelt flour and the rich, creamy goodness of Manchego cheese. Imagine thin, crisp crackers, adorned with the earthy richness of spelt and the savory notes of aged Manchego—a snack that not only satisfies your cravings but also celebrates the art of pairing flavors.

At their core, these crackers are a celebration of spelt flour, known for its nutty, slightly sweet flavor and nutritional benefits. The addition of finely grated Manchego cheese provides depth and a hint of sharpness, elevating these crackers to a new level of deliciousness.

Enjoy Manchego Spelt Crackers as a versatile and sophisticated snack, perfect for pairing with wine, enjoying with a cheese platter, or serving with your favorite dips and spreads. Their unique flavor profile adds an elegant touch to any gathering or moment of indulgence.

Creating these crackers is a culinary adventure that combines the nuttiness of spelt with the richness of Manchego cheese. The dough is carefully mixed, rolled thin, and cut into perfect squares, creating crackers that are as visually appealing as they are delicious.

The result is Manchego Spelt Crackers that capture the essence of gourmet snacking and the joy of savoring the complementary flavors of spelt and Manchego in every bite. Each cracker is a reminder of the artistry of flavor pairing and the simple pleasure of indulging in a sophisticated snack that combines the magic of these two ingredients—a true delight for the palate.

- 60 g (½ cup) spelt flour
- 60 g (½ cup) all-purpose flour
- 3 g (½ tsp) coarse sea salt or Himalayan salt
- ½ tsp paprika
- 35 g (⅓ cup) grated Manchego cheese
- 75 g (5 tbsp) unsalted butter, cold, cut into pieces
- 226 g (1 cup) sourdough discard
- 14 g (1 tbsp) water

1. Preheat the oven to 200°C. Line a 45 x 33–cm baking sheet with parchment paper.
2. Whisk together the spelt flour, all-purpose flour, salt, paprika and Manchego cheese. Using a pastry cutter or two butter knives, incorporate the butter into the flour mixture until the mixture resembles coarse crumbs. Stir the sourdough discard and water into the mixture until they're fully incorporated. Gather the dough into a ball and squeeze it a few times to bring it together. Divide the dough in half.
3. Working with one portion at a time, place the dough between two pieces of parchment paper. Use a rolling pin to roll the dough out until it is 3 mm thick. With a 5-cm fluted biscuit cutter, cut as many crackers out of the dough as you can. Using a pastry scraper, transfer the dough disks onto the lined baking sheet. Repeat with the remaining dough and reroll the scraps. Fill the baking sheets and bake as many crackers as you can.
4. Bake the crackers for about 15 minutes, until they're a medium golden brown. Remove them from the oven and cool right on the pan.
5. When the crackers are cool, store them in an airtight container at room temperature for up to 1 month.

Vanilla Raspberries Bread

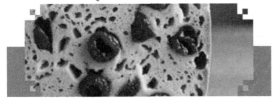

Prep time: 10 minutes | Cook time: 1 hour | Makes 1 loaf

Vanilla Raspberry Bread is a delightful fusion of the aromatic warmth of vanilla and the vibrant sweetness of raspberries. Imagine slices of this golden loaf, each one infused with the comforting aroma of vanilla and studded with plump, juicy raspberries—a bread that not only satisfies your sweet tooth but also captures the essence of fruity indulgence.

At its core, this bread features the warmth of vanilla extract, which provides a fragrant, slightly sweet flavor. The result is a bread that's both comforting and exciting, perfect for breakfast, brunch, or a sweet snack.

Creating this bread is a culinary adventure that combines the art of baking with the flavors of vanilla and raspberries. fruit-studded crumb, ready to be sliced and savored.

The result is Vanilla Raspberry Bread that captures the essence of sweet indulgence. Each slice is a reminder of the magic of baking and the simple pleasure of enjoying a loaf that combines the richness of vanilla with the sweetness of raspberries—a true delight for the senses.

- 240g white flour
- 5g baking powder
- 150g erythritol
- 2.5g salt
- 1 egg
- 180ml almond milk
- 60ml ghee, melted
- 240g raspberries
- 10ml vanilla extract
- 60ml vegetable oil

1. In a bowl, mix together the white flour, baking powder, salt, erythritol, egg, almond milk, melted ghee, vanilla extract, and vegetable oil. Stir until all the ingredients are well combined.
2. Gently fold in the raspberries into the batter.
3. Pour the batter into a lined loaf pan.
4. Bake in a preheated oven at 350 degrees F (175 degrees C) for approximately 1 hour or until a toothpick inserted into the center comes out clean.
5. Once baked, remove the raspberry bread from the oven and allow it to cool in the pan for a few minutes.
6. Transfer the bread to a wire rack to cool completely.
7. Once cooled, slice the raspberry bread and serve. Enjoy your delicious raspberry bread with the sweet-tart flavor of raspberries!

Rum Raisin Bread Pudding

Prep time: 5 minutes | Prep time: 5 minutes | Cook time: 15 minutes | Serves 4to 6

Rum Raisin Bread Pudding is a luscious and indulgent dessert that marries the rich, comforting qualities of bread pudding with the sophisticated flavors of rum-soaked raisins. Imagine a warm, custardy pudding, studded with plump raisins that have been steeped in aromatic rum—a dessert that not only delights your taste buds but also adds a touch of elegance to any occasion.

At its heart, this dessert showcases the magical transformation of simple ingredients. Stale bread, milk, eggs, sugar, and vanilla are combined to create .The addition of rum-soaked raisins infuses each spoonful with a delightful warmth and depth of flavor.

Creating this dessert is a culinary adventure that involves the art of blending textures and flavors. Baking it to perfection results in a dessert that captures the essence of homemade comfort and the simple joy of savoring a dessert that's both rustic and refined.

- 2 cups (480 ml) whole milk
- 6 large eggs
- ¼ cup (50 g) sugar, plus extra for sprinkling
- Pinch of salt
- 2 tbsp (28 g) unsalted butter, plus more for coating
- 2 tbsp (30 ml) dark rum
- 6 slices day-old everyday sourdough, cubed, about 6 cups (240 g)
- Handful of raisins or currants
- 2 tbsp (30 ml) caramel sauce
- Powdered sugar, for sprinkling

1. For the custard, gently warm the milk in a small saucepan over low heat. Meanwhile, whisk the eggs, sugar, and salt in a medium bowl. Slowly pour the warm milk into the egg mixture, whisking continuously to combine. Then pour the custard back into the pan.
2. Adjust the heat to medium-low and cook the custard until slightly thick, stirring often to prevent it from scorching on the bottom of the pan, about 10 to 15 minutes. The final texture should be similar to heavy cream, but not thick like pudding. Stir in the butter to melt and add the rum. Strain the custard through a fine-mesh sieve.
3. Add the bread cubes to a large bowl, along with a handful of raisins. Pour the warm custard over the bread. Toss well to combine. Let the mixture sit for at least 30 minutes to absorb the custard.

Jewish Bread

Prep time: 2 hours and 10 minutes | Cook time: 1 hour |

Makes 1 bread

Jewish bread holds a special place in culinary history, interweaving tradition, symbolism, and exquisite flavors. These diverse bread types aren't merely staples; they're living connections to centuries of heritage, lovingly prepared in homes and bakeries around the world.

Challah: the braided, sweet challah is not just bread; it's a centerpiece at Shabbat tables, symbolizing unity and blessings. Its tender crumb, often sweetened with honey, pairs wonderfully with various dishes.

Matzah: During Passover, matzah's unleavened simplicity reminds us of the haste during the Exodus. Its crisp, striped appearance carries profound historical significance.

Bagels: Iconic in Jewish cuisine, bagels offer a delightful chewy interior and crispy crust. They're an ideal vessel for cream cheese, smoked salmon, and countless toppings.

Rye Bread: Jewish rye bread boasts a hearty, tangy flavor and dense texture, elevating classic deli sandwiches like pastrami or corned beef.

Beyond their historical and religious roles, these breads offer culinary versatility. Challah can be transformed into decadent French toast; matzah can be a canvas for inventive toppings; bagels can host a myriad of spreads, and rye bread can anchor gourmet sandwiches.

While enjoying Jewish bread, remember that each bite carries stories of resilience, faith, and community. These breads connect us to our roots and invite us to savor the artistry and symbolism baked into each delicious loaf.

- 1 egg yolk, whisked
- 1 egg white, whisked
- 10 g salt
- 240 ml warm water
- 120 ml honey
- 30 ml olive oil
- 480 g white flour
- 10 g bread machine yeast

1. In your bread machine, add the white flour, bread machine yeast, salt, warm water, honey, olive oil, whisked egg yolk, and whisked egg white.
2. Set the bread machine to the "Basil" cycle and select the desired crust color. Start the machine.
3. When the final rise is done, set the machine on pause, and carefully transfer the dough to a floured working surface.
4. Divide the dough into 3 equal parts. Roll each part into long ropes and braid them together. Tuck the ends to secure the braid.
5. Place the braided bread back into the bread machine pan.
6. Continue the bread machine cycle until it's finished.
7. Once the bread is done, remove it from the machine, and allow it to cool.
8. Slice and serve your freshly baked braided honey bread.

Cuban Medianoche Sourdough Bread

Prep time: 4 hours 15 minutes | Cook time: 4 hours 40 minutes | Makes 2 free-form loaves

Cuban Medianoche Sourdough Bread is a delightful fusion of the tangy allure of sourdough and the savory charm of the Cuban Medianoche sandwich. Imagine slices of this golden loaf, each one infused with the unmistakable tang of sourdough, ready to cradle the classic fillings of roasted pork, ham, Swiss cheese, pickles, and mustard—a bread that not only pays homage to Cuban cuisine but also adds a unique twist with sourdough sophistication.

At its core, this sourdough bread features a chewy, tangy crumb that complements the savory and zesty flavors of the Medianoche sandwich fillings. The dough is prepared with care, allowing the sourdough starter to impart its characteristic tang and complexity to the bread.

Cuban Medianoche Sourdough Bread is the perfect foundation for crafting authentic Medianoche sandwiches. Its tangy profile enhances the overall experience, offering a delightful contrast to the savory meats and the zing of the pickles and mustard. It's a bread that elevates this classic Cuban sandwich to a new level of deliciousness.

Creating this bread is a culinary journey that combines the art of sourdough fermentation with the flavors of Cuban cuisine. The sourdough starter is incorporated into the dough, allowing it to rise and develop its signature tangy flavor. Baking it to perfection results in a loaf that captures the essence of both sourdough sophistication and the tradition of Cuban Medianoche sandwiches.

Each slice is a reminder of the rich culinary heritage of Cuba and the joy of savoring the tangy twist of sourdough in a classic sandwich that embodies the spirit of Cuban cuisine. Cuban Medianoche Sourdough Bread is an invitation to indulge in the flavors of the Caribbean with a unique sourdough twist—a true culinary delight for any sandwich enthusiast.

Tools Needed:
stand mixer, baking stone, parchment paper, baking pan, bread lame or very sharp knife

For Activating the Starter:
- 135 grams (1/2 cup) sourdough starter
- 120 milliliters (1/2 cup) lukewarm (32°C to 38°C) pure filtered or bottled water
- 115 grams (1 cup) whole-wheat flour

For the Bread Dough:
- 2 1/4 teaspoons active dry yeast
- 2 teaspoons sugar
- 180 milliliters (3/4 cup) room temperature (24°C) pure filtered or bottled water
- 3 tablespoons good quality lard or butter, melted and cooled
- 2 teaspoons fine sea salt
- 300 grams (2 1/2 cups) unbleached all-purpose flour or unbleached bread flour, plus more for dusting
- 270 grams (1 cup) active whole-wheat sourdough starter
- Olive oil or nonstick cooking spray, for preparing the bowl
- 2 cups ice cubes

To Activate the Starter:
1. At least 6 to 12 hours before making the dough, in a medium bowl, combine the starter, lukewarm water, and flour, completely incorporating the ingredients into the starter. Loosely cover and let sit on the counter until ready to use.

To Make the Bread Dough:
2. In the bowl of a stand mixer, or a large bowl, whisk the yeast and sugar. Add the room temperature water and whisk again. Let sit for at least 15 minutes.
3. Add the lard, salt, flour, and active starter to the bowl. Attach the dough hook and mix together on low speed, or stir by hand with a large wooden spoon.
4. Flour a breadboard or clean work surface and turn the dough out onto it. Knead the dough until it forms a firm ball. Use more flour, if necessary, to keep the dough from being overly sticky. Just don't add too much.
5. Generously coat a large bowl with olive oil and transfer the dough to it, turning to coat all sides. Cover the bowl with plastic wrap and set in a warm place to rise for 2 hours.
6. Flour a breadboard or clean work surface and turn the dough out onto it. Divide the dough in half. Shape the dough into two free-form loaves. Roll one piece into a log about 30 centimeters long. Tuck the ends under and roll the dough until it's smooth. Repeat with the other loaf. Cover with a clean floured kitchen towel and let the loaves proof for 1½ hours, or until they double in size.

Chapter 7

Sweet Recipes

Blackberry Avocado Bread

Prep time: 10 minutes | Cook time: 50 minutes | Makes 1 loaf

Blackberry Avocado Bread is a delightful fusion of vibrant, juicy blackberries and the creamy goodness of ripe avocados. Imagine slices of this golden loaf, each one generously studded with bursts of sweet blackberries, and infused with the subtle richness of avocados—a bread that not only satisfies your sweet cravings but also offers a wealth of natural nutrients.

At its core, this bread celebrates the natural sweetness and vibrant color of blackberries.Buttery flavor that pairs perfectly with the tartness of the berries. The result is a bread that's both visually stunning and rich in flavor.

Blackberry Avocado Bread is a versatile treat that can be enjoyed as a wholesome breakfast option, a sweet snack, or a delightful dessert. Whether served plain or with a dollop of whipped cream, each bite offers a burst of berry goodness and the subtle creaminess of avocados.

Each bite of Blackberry Avocado Bread is a reminder of the magic of incorporating fresh fruits and natural ingredients into baking. It's a bread that not only satisfies your palate but also nourishes your body with the vibrant colors and flavors of nature—a true delight for those seeking a balance of indulgence and nutrition in their bread.

- 240g white flour
- 2 ripe avocados, peeled, pitted, and mashed
- 150g blackberries
- 80ml honey
- 5g baking soda
- 5g baking powder
- 5g salt
- 5g ground nutmeg
- 5ml vanilla extract
- 2 eggs

1. In a mixing bowl, combine the white flour with the honey, baking soda, baking powder, salt, and ground nutmeg. Mix these dry ingredients together.
2. In a separate bowl, mash the ripe avocados until smooth.
3. Add the mashed avocados, blackberries, vanilla extract, and eggs to the dry ingredient mixture. Stir everything together until well combined.
4. Preheat your oven to 350 degrees F (175 degrees C).
5. Pour the batter into a greased or lined loaf pan.

Light and Airy Waffles

Prep time: 10 minutes | Cook time: 20 minutes | Makes about 6 waffles

Light and Airy Waffles are a delightful morning indulgence, offering a harmonious blend of crispy exteriors and tender, fluffy interiors. Imagine a plate piled high with golden waffles, each one with a delicate, airy texture that's just waiting to be drizzled with syrup or adorned with fresh fruit—a breakfast treat that not only satisfies your morning cravings but also embodies the art of perfect waffle-making.

At their core, these waffles celebrate the simplicity of classic waffle ingredients—flour, eggs, milk, and a touch of sweetness.The result is a waffle that's both comforting and sophisticated, perfect for leisurely weekend breakfasts or special occasions.

Creating these waffles is a culinary adventure that involves the art of waffle-making and the careful balance of ingredients.Baking them to a golden perfection results in waffles that capture the essence of classic breakfast comfort and the simple pleasure of savoring a perfectly executed waffle.

Each bite of Light and Airy Waffles is a reminder of the magic of mastering the waffle iron and the satisfaction of indulging in a breakfast that embodies the ideal balance of crispy and tender—an exquisite treat for those who appreciate the art of waffle craftsmanship.

- 470 ml (2 cups) active starter
- 2 eggs, yolks separated
- 60 ml (¼ cup) milk
- 10 ml (2 tsp) butter, melted and cooled slightly
- 5 ml (1 tsp) granulated sugar
- 5 ml (1 tsp) salt
- 120 to 240 ml (½ to 1 cup) unbleached all-purpose flour

1. In a medium mixing bowl, stir together the starter, egg yolks, milk, melted butter, sugar, and salt. Add enough flour, a bit at a time, to attain a pourable but thick batter and mix well to ensure the batter is smooth and free of lumps. Cover the bowl and let it sit at room temperature for 1½ hours.
2. Beat the egg whites until soft peaks form, and then gently fold them into the batter.
3. Cook the waffles according to your waffle iron's directions. Top the waffles with butter, syrup, jam, fruit, or sweetened whipped cream.

Sourdough Gingerbread Cookies

Prep time: 20 minutes | Cook time: 15 minutes | Serves 1

Sourdough Gingerbread Cookies offer a delightful blend of the warm, comforting spices of traditional gingerbread and the tangy sophistication of sourdough. Imagine gingerbread cookies, richly spiced and beautifully shaped, with a subtle tang that elevates their flavor—a holiday treat that not only captures the essence of festive baking but also adds a unique twist with sourdough complexity.

At their core, these gingerbread cookies showcase the magic of sourdough starter, which imparts a delightful tanginess and depth of flavor to the dough. The result is a cookie that's both aromatic and intriguing, perfect for holiday gatherings and gifting.

Sourdough Gingerbread Cookies are perfect for celebrating the holiday season. Cut them into festive shapes and decorate them with icing or enjoy them plain, allowing their rich, complex flavors to shine through. Each bite is a reminder of the joy of holiday baking and the simple pleasure of savoring cookies that balance tradition with innovation.

Creating these cookies is a culinary adventure that combines the art of baking with the magic of sourdough fermentation. The sourdough starter is incorporated into the dough, allowing it to rise and develop its signature tangy flavor. Once baked to perfection, the cookies emerge with a tender, spiced crumb and a depth of flavor that's sure to delight.

Experience the magic of the season with our Sourdough Gingerbread Cookies. Each cookie is a sweet reminder of the joyous moments spent in the kitchen during the festive season. Our gingerbread cookies are a harmonious blend of cherished traditions and contemporary culinary innovation, making them the perfect choice for sharing holiday happiness.

- 360 g all-purpose flour
- 4 g ground ginger
- 7.5 g baking soda
- 4.5 g ground cinnamon
- 0.45 g salt
- 0.5 g allspice
- 0.25 g ground cloves
- 0.25 g ground cardamom
- 200 g brown sugar
- 120 g sourdough discard, 100% hydration
- 113 g unsalted butter, room temperature
- 85 g molasses
- 1 large egg
- 5 g vanilla extract

1. In a large mixing bowl, combine the flour, ground ginger, baking soda, cinnamon, salt, allspice, cloves, and cardamom.
2. In another bowl, mix the brown sugar and butter. Beat this mixture on medium speed for about three minutes, or until it's light and fluffy.
3. Add the sourdough discard, molasses, egg, and vanilla extract to the sugar-butter mixture. Mix until everything is well combined.
4. Gradually add the flour mixture to the wet ingredients, stirring until just incorporated. Be careful not to overmix; you want a smooth dough without any lumps.
5. Divide the dough into two equal portions and shape each into a disc. Wrap them in plastic wrap and chill in the refrigerator for at least 4 hours, or preferably overnight.

Blueberry Pancakes

Prep time: 10 minutes | Cook time: 20 minutes | Serves 8

Blueberry Pancakes are a delightful breakfast classic, where fluffy pancakes are generously studded with plump, juicy blueberries, creating a symphony of flavors and textures in every bite. Imagine a stack of golden pancakes, their edges slightly crisp and their centers tender and bursting with sweet blueberries—a breakfast treat that not only satisfies your morning cravings but also celebrates the simple pleasure of home-cooked goodness.

At their heart, these pancakes highlight the sweet and tart essence of blueberries. The result is a pancake that's both comforting and exciting, perfect for leisurely weekend breakfasts or a quick and delicious morning meal.

Enjoy Blueberry Pancakes with a drizzle of maple syrup, a dollop of whipped cream, or a sprinkle of powdered sugar. Their sweet and fruity aroma will fill your kitchen, inviting you to savor the simple joys of homemade breakfast.

Each bite of Blueberry Pancakes is a reminder of the magic of combining classic pancake ingredients with the freshness and sweetness of blueberries—a true delight for breakfast enthusiasts seeking a burst of berry bliss in every mouthful.

- 355 ml (1½ cups) starter (discard is fine)
- 235 ml (1 cup) milk (room temperature if you have the time)
- 2 eggs (room temperature if you have the time)
- 60 ml (¼ cup) butter, melted and cooled slightly
- 5 ml (1 tsp) vanilla extract
- 180 g (1½ cups) unbleached all-purpose flour
- 5 ml (1 tsp) baking soda
- 5 ml (1 tsp) baking powder
- 2.5 ml (½ tsp) salt
- 1 pint blueberries (you can use fresh, canned and drained, or frozen berries that have been thawed and drained)

1. In a large mixing bowl, whisk together the starter, milk, eggs, melted butter, and vanilla extract. Mix in the dry ingredients one at a time until well blended. Gently fold in the blueberries.
2. Pour ¼ cup (60 ml) of batter per pancake into a heated and greased pan or skillet. Cook for about 3 minutes on one side until you see bubbles forming on the surface. Flip the pancakes and cook the second side until done, about 2 minutes or until they are golden brown.

Fast Coconut and Cherry Tea Loaf

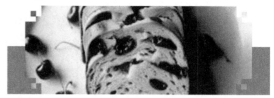

Prep time: 10 minutes | Cook time: 2 hours minutes | Serves 4

The Fast Coconut and Cherry Tea Loaf is a delightful treat that offers a quick and easy way to enjoy the flavors of coconut and cherries in a moist and tender loaf. Imagine slices of this golden bread, each one bursting with the sweet richness of cherries and the tropical allure of coconut—a baked delight that not only satisfies your sweet cravings but also caters to your need for convenience.

At its core, this loaf showcases the simplicity of quick bread-making, where the batter comes together swiftly. The cherries provide a burst of sweetness and the coconut adds a hint of tropical indulgence. The result is a loaf that's both comforting and convenient.

Each bite of the Fast Coconut and Cherry Tea Loaf is a reminder of the. It's a loaf that celebrates the convenience of quick breads while embracing the delightful combination of cherries and coconut—a true delight for those seeking a speedy and satisfying treat.

- 100 g (½ cup) starter (fed, unfed or discarded)
- 400 g (1¾ cups) coconut milk
- 400 g (2½ cups) white spelt flour, plain or all-purpose flour
- 200 g (1¼ cups) glacé (candied) cherries
- 100 g (¾ cup) dried cranberries
- 50 g (½ cup) shredded coconut
- 30 g (⅛ cup) runny honey
- 1 large egg
- 7 g (1 tsp) baking soda
- 4 g (½ tsp) baking powder

1. In a medium-sized mixing bowl, combine all the ingredients. Mix them well to form a lumpy, thick batter, ensuring no dry flour is left. It will fill the bowl.
2. Spoon the mixture into your prepared loaf pan.
3. When you are ready to bake, decide whether you would like to bake in a preheated oven or from a cold start. If preheating, set the oven to 180°C for convection or 200°C for conventional.
4. If you preheated the oven, bake the loaf uncovered for 50 to 60 minutes, or until a metal skewer or thin knife inserted into the center comes out clean. If you are using a cold start, place the uncovered pan of dough in the oven, set the temperature as above and set a timer for 60 minutes. Bake it for the allotted time, or until a metal skewer or thin knife inserted into the center comes out clean.

Amish Friendship Chocolate Chip Bread

**Prep time: 10 minutes | Cook time: 20 minutes | Makes
2 loaves**

Amish Friendship Chocolate Chip Bread is a heartwarming delight, born from the tradition of sharing and nurturing friendships through homemade treats. Imagine a loaf of chocolate-studded bread, rich in flavor and history, made with love and shared among friends—a bread that not only satisfies your sweet tooth but also carries the warmth of meaningful connections.

At its core, this bread features a sweet and moist bread base enriched with chocolate chips, creating a comforting and indulgent treat. As the starter is shared, so are stories, memories, and the joy of friendship.

Amish Friendship Chocolate Chip Bread is not just a delicious treat; it's a symbol of camaraderie and care. Baking it and sharing it with friends and loved ones is a cherished tradition that celebrates the bonds we form through food.

Creating this bread is a culinary adventure that involves nurturing a sourdough-like starter, known as the "Amish Friendship Bread Starter."Chocolate chip bread. Baking it to a golden perfection results in a loaf that captures the essence of homemade comfort and the sentiment of sharing and friendship.

Each slice of Amish Friendship Chocolate Chip Bread is a reminder of the magic of connecting through food and the joy of nurturing meaningful relationships. It's a bread that carries the sweetness of chocolate chips and the warmth of friendship in every bite—a true delight for those who appreciate the heartwarming traditions of the Amish kitchen.

Bread Dough:
- 240 ml (1 cup) Amish Friendship Bread starter
- 3 eggs
- 240 ml (1 cup) oil
- 120 ml (½ cup) milk
- 2.5 ml (½ tsp) vanilla extract
- 2 small boxes instant chocolate pudding (96g each)
- 240 g (2 cups) unbleached all-purpose flour
- 200 g (1 cup) granulated sugar
- 60 g (½ cup) cocoa powder
- 7.5 ml (1½ tsp) baking powder
- 2.5 ml (½ tsp) salt
- 2.5 ml (½ tsp) baking soda
- 180 g (1 cup) chocolate chips, tossed with 15-30 ml (1-2 tablespoons) flour to help them "float" while baking

Dusting:
- 100 g (½ cup) granulated sugar
- 2.5 ml (½ tsp) cocoa powder

1. Preheat the oven to 325°F (165°C).
2. In a large mixing bowl, add the starter, eggs, oil, milk, and vanilla extract; mix well.
3. In another bowl, whisk together the chocolate pudding mixes, flour, sugar, cocoa powder, baking powder, salt, and baking soda. Add the flour mixture to the starter mixture and stir well to blend. Add the prepared chocolate chips and gently mix to combine.
4. In a small bowl, mix the sugar and cocoa powder for dusting.
5. Grease 2 loaf pans. Dust the prepared pans Pour in the batter evenly between both loaf pans and sprinkle the remaining cocoa and sugar mixture on top of the batter.

Banana Nut Muffins

Prep time: 10 minutes | Cook time: 20 minutes | Makes 12 muffins

Banana Nut Muffins are a comforting and flavorful treat that combines the natural sweetness of ripe bananas with the crunch of toasted nuts. Imagine moist, golden muffins, each one brimming with the goodness of mashed bananas and the delightful nuttiness of walnuts or pecans—a baked delight that not only satisfies your cravings but also celebrates the timeless appeal of homemade goodness.

At their core, these muffins celebrate the simplicity of classic muffin ingredients—flour, ripe bananas, eggs, sugar, and a handful of toasted nuts. The magic happens when these elements come together, creating a moist, tender crumb with a hint of banana sweetness and the earthy, hearty flavor of nuts.

Banana Nut Muffins are the perfect addition to your morning routine or an anytime snack. Each bite is a reminder of the joy of homemade baking and the comforting embrace of a well-crafted muffin.

Creating these muffins is a culinary adventure that involves the art of muffin-making and the careful incorporation of mashed bananas and toasted nuts. Baking them to a golden brown results in muffins that capture the essence of classic comfort and the simple pleasure of savoring a homemade treat.

Each bite of Banana Nut Muffins is a reminder of the magic of combining everyday ingredients to create a timeless classic. It's a muffin that embodies the natural sweetness of bananas and the satisfying crunch of nuts—a true delight for those who appreciate the heartwarming simplicity of homemade baked goods.

- 180 g unbleached all-purpose flour
- 5 ml (1 tsp) baking soda
- 2.5 ml (½ tsp) salt
- 2.5 ml (½ tsp) ground cinnamon
- 115 g (½ cup or 1 stick) butter, softened
- 50 g (¼ cup) granulated sugar
- 3 very ripe bananas
- 2 eggs
- 5 ml (1 tsp) vanilla extract
- 240 ml (1 cup) starter (active or discard)
- 90 g (¾ cup) walnuts, chopped

1. Grease a 12-cup muffin tin or use paper cups that have been slightly sprayed with oil.
2. In a small mixing bowl, whisk together the flour, baking soda, salt, and cinnamon; set aside for now.
3. In a large mixing bowl, cream together the butter and sugar (use a hand mixer) until the mixture is well combined and smooth. Add the bananas and beat with the hand mixer until the bananas are thoroughly mashed and well combined. Add the eggs and vanilla and beat again until mixed completely. Add the starter and either mix on low just until combined or gently stir by hand. Fold in the walnuts. Evenly divide the batter into the prepared muffin tin.
4. Preheat the oven to 350°F (175°C) while the muffins rest for 15 minutes. Bake for 25 to 30 minutes or until a toothpick inserted into the middle comes out clean.
5. Cool the muffins in the tin for 10 minutes and then loosen the muffins by running a knife around the edges and place them on a wire rack to continue cooling. If you used paper liners, leave the muffins inside them and place them on a wire rack to cool.

Blackberry Sourdough Bread Cobbler

Prep time: 10 minutes | Cook time: 20 minutes | Serves 4 to 6

Blackberry Sourdough Bread Cobbler is a delightful fusion of the tangy allure of sourdough and the sweet, fruity goodness of blackberries. Imagine a warm, bubbling cobbler, its golden crust dotted with sourdough bread cubes and crowned with plump, juicy blackberries—a dessert that not only satisfies your sweet tooth but also adds a unique twist with the tangy sophistication of sourdough.

At its core, this cobbler highlights the magic of sourdough starter, which infuses the bread cubes with a delightful tang and complexity of flavor. The result is a cobbler that's both rustic and refined, perfect for sharing with loved ones on any occasion.

Blackberry Sourdough Bread Cobbler is best enjoyed warm, either on its own or with a scoop of vanilla ice cream. That invites you to savor the simple joys of homemade dessert.

Creating this cobbler is a culinary adventure that combines the art of baking with the flavors of blackberries and sourdough. The result is a dessert that captures the essence of rustic comfort and the unique twist of sourdough sophistication.

- 600 g blackberries
- 15 ml (3 tsp) cornstarch
- 135 g (⅔ cup) brown sugar
- 50 g (¼ cup) granulated sugar
- 115 g (½ cup or 1 stick) butter, melted and cooled slightly
- 1 egg, beaten
- 10 ml (2 tsp) flour
- 2.5 ml (½ tsp) ground cinnamon
- 360 g (4 cups) cubed sourdough bread, about 2.5 cm (1 inch) squares

1. Preheat the oven to 350°F (175°C). Butter or grease a 9 × 9-inch (23 × 23 cm) baking dish.
2. In a large bowl, mix the blackberries and cornstarch. Spread the fruit mixture evenly on the bottom of the prepared baking dish.
3. In a small bowl, mix the sugars, melted butter, beaten egg, flour, and cinnamon until well combined and smooth.
4. Place the bread cubes on top of the blackberry mixture, pressing down gently and trying for an even top. Drizzle the sugar and butter mixture evenly over the top of the bread cubes.

Southern Sourdough Biscuits

Prep time: 15 minutes | Cook time: 25 minutes | Makes 8 biscuits

Southern Sourdough Biscuits are a delightful fusion of the traditional Southern biscuit and the tangy sophistication of sourdough. Imagine biscuits that are at once tender, flaky, and kissed with a subtle tang—a Southern classic that not only satisfies your cravings but also adds a unique twist with the complexity of sourdough.

At their core, these biscuits showcase the magic of sourdough starter, which imparts a delightful tanginess and depth of flavor to the dough. The result is a biscuit that's both rustic and refined, perfect for breakfast, brunch, or as a side dish for Southern comfort meals.

Enjoy Southern Sourdough Biscuits warm, slathered with butter, drizzled with honey, or paired with country gravy. Their rich, buttery aroma and tender texture make them a versatile addition to any Southern-style meal.

Each bite of Southern Sourdough Biscuits is a reminder of the magic of combining Southern tradition with the tangy allure of sourdough. It's a biscuit that embodies the timeless charm of Southern cooking while adding a layer of complexity and flavor—a true delight for those seeking a taste of the South with a touch of tangy sophistication.

Tools Needed:
baking sheet, 2½-inch biscuit or cookie cutter, rolling pin

For Activating the Starter:
- 68 grams (1/4 cup) sourdough starter
- 120 milliliters (1/2 cup) lukewarm (32°C to 38°C) pure filtered or bottled water
- 115 grams (1 cup) whole-wheat flour

To Activate the Starter:
1. At least 6 to 12 hours before making the dough, in a medium bowl, combine the starter, lukewarm water, and flour, completely incorporating the ingredients into the starter. Loosely cover and let sit on the counter until ready to use.

Sticky Date, Walnut, and Orange

Prep time: 5 minutes | Cook time: 15 minutes | Makes 1 loaf

Sticky Date, Walnut, and Orange Bread is a harmonious blend of luscious dates, earthy walnuts, and the bright citrusy notes of oranges. Imagine slices of this golden loaf, each one boasting tender bits of sticky dates, crunchy walnuts, and the refreshing zest of oranges—a bread that not only satisfies your sweet cravings but also delights your palate with a symphony of textures and flavors.

At its core, this bread celebrates the natural sweetness and chewiness of dates, balanced by the earthy depth of toasted walnuts. The addition of orange zest and juice provides a zesty brightness that elevates the flavor profile. The result is a bread that's both comforting and exciting, perfect for breakfast, brunch, or a sweet snack.

Enjoy Sticky Date, Walnut, and Orange Bread toasted and lightly buttered for a simple pleasure, or pair it with a cup of tea or coffee to enhance its citrusy undertones. Its sweet and aromatic aroma will fill your kitchen, inviting you to savor the simple joys of homemade baked goods.

Creating this bread is a culinary adventure that involves the art of blending textures and flavors. The dates and walnuts are carefully folded into the batter, ensuring even distribution and bursts of sweetness and crunch in every slice. Baking it to a golden perfection results in a loaf that captures the essence of natural ingredients and the simple joy of savoring a slice packed with goodness.

Each bite of Sticky Date, Walnut, and Orange Bread is a reminder of the magic of combining diverse ingredients to create a bread that's both indulgent and wholesome. It's a bread that celebrates the richness of dates, the nutty crunch of walnuts, and the refreshing brightness of oranges—a true delight for those seeking a symphony of flavors in their homemade bread.

Dough:
- 50 g (¼ cup) bubbly, active starter
- 350 g (1⅓ cups plus 2 tbsp) warm water
- 100 g (¾ cup plus 1 tbsp) whole wheat flour
- 100 g (¾ cup plus 1 tbsp) bread flour
- 200 g (1⅓ cups) all-purpose flour
- 9 g (1½ tsp) fine sea salt

Fillings:
- 65 g (½ cup) chopped walnuts
- 6 medjool dates, pitted and diced into small pieces
- zest of 4 clementines or 1 large orange

Make the Dough:
1. In a large bowl, whisk the starter and water together with a fork. Add the flours and salt. Combine to form a rough dough, mopping up any dry bits of flour as you go. Cover with a damp towel and let rest for 45 minutes to 1 hour. Replenish your starter with fresh flour and water, and store according to preference.
2. Meanwhile, warm a nonstick pan over low heat. Toast the walnuts until fragrant, stirring occasionally, about 3 to 4 minutes. Once cool enough to handle, chop into small pieces.

Add the Fillings:
1. After the dough has rested, add the toasted walnuts and dates to the bowl. Zest the clementines into the dough. Gently knead the dough to incorporate, about 1 minute.

Bulk Rise:
1. Cover the dough with a damp towel and let rise at room temperature, 21°C, until double in size, about 8 to 10 hours or more.

Shape:
1. Remove the dough onto a lightly floured work surface. Shape the dough into an oval and let rest for 5 to 10 minutes. Meanwhile, generously dust a 25-cm oval proofing basket with flour. With floured hands, gently cup the dough and pull it toward you to tighten its shape. Place the dough into your basket, seam side up.

Second Rise:
1. Cover the dough and let rest until puffy but not fully risen, about 30 minutes to 1 hour.
2. Preheat your oven to 230°C. Cut a sheet of parchment paper to fit the size of your baking pot.

Score:
1. Place the parchment over the dough and invert the basket to release. Make a long cut down the length of the dough, using the tip of a small knife or razor blade. Use the parchment to transfer the dough into the baking pot.

Bake:
1. Bake the dough on the center rack for 20 minutes, covered. Remove the lid, and continue to bake for 30 minutes. Lift the bread out of the pot, and finish baking directly on the oven rack for the last 10 minutes. Transfer to a wire rack and cool for 1 hour before slicing.
2. This loaf will stay fresh up to 1 to 2 days, stored at room temperature in a plastic bag.

Chapter 8

Rustic Recipes

Mexican Rustic Loaf

Prep time: 2 hours and 10 minutes | Cook time: 20 minutes | Makes 2 loaves

The Mexican Rustic Loaf is a delightful fusion of traditional Mexican flavors and the rustic charm of homemade bread. Imagine a golden loaf, its crust kissed with a hint of cornmeal, and its crumb boasting the warmth of Mexican spices—a bread that not only satisfies your cravings but also transports your palate to the heart of Mexico.

Savor the Mexican Rustic Loaf with a drizzle of olive oil and a sprinkle of sea salt for a simple pleasure, or use it as the foundation for tortas, sandwiches, or dipping into a bowl of chili. Its aroma and flavor will transport you to the bustling streets and vibrant markets of Mexico, where every bite is a culinary adventure.

Creating this bread is a culinary journey that involves the art of breadmaking and the careful blending of spices. Baking it to a golden perfection results in a loaf that captures the essence of Mexican cuisine and the simple joy of savoring a slice that's both rustic and flavorful.

Each bite of the Mexican Rustic Loaf is a reminder of the magic of incorporating spices into breadmaking and the satisfaction of savoring a loaf that marries the rich traditions of Mexican cooking with the rustic allure of homemade bread—a true delight for those seeking a flavorful fiesta in every bite.

- 480 g white flour
- 135 g sugar
- 235 ml milk
- 115 g butter
- 10 g dry yeast
- 5 g cinnamon powder
- 1 egg
- 5 ml vanilla extract

1. In a large bowl, mix the flour with the sugar, milk, and the other ingredients. Stir until you obtain a dough, then cover and leave it aside for 2 hours to allow it to rise.
2. After the dough has risen, shape it into loaves and place them on a baking sheet lined with parchment paper.
3. Preheat your oven to 220°C (435°F) and bake the loaves for approximately 20 minutes or until they turn golden brown.
4. Allow the loaves to cool down, then slice and serve.

Russian Bread

Prep time: 3 hours and 10 minutes | Cook time: 40 minutes | Makes 2 loaves

Russian Bread is a celebration of Russia's rich culinary heritage, offering a hearty and flavorful slice of tradition. Imagine a dense, dark loaf, boasting a robust, earthy flavor with a hint of molasses sweetness—a bread that not only satisfies your cravings but also reflects the resilience and warmth of Russian culture.

At its core, this bread embraces the simplicity of traditional Russian breadmaking, using rye flour as its base. Russian Bread is a staple that has nourished generations and remains an integral part of Russian cuisine.

Creating this bread is a culinary journey that involves the art of breadmaking and the respect for time-honored traditions.Baking it to a deep, dark brown results in a loaf that captures the essence of Russian cuisine and the simple joy of savoring a slice steeped in history and culture.

Each bite of Russian Bread is a reminder of the magic of preserving culinary traditions and the satisfaction of savoring a bread that's both hearty and timeless. This vast and diverse country—a true delight for those seeking a taste of Russia's culinary heritage.

- 360 g white flour
- 470 ml warm water
- 30 ml cider vinegar
- 2.5 g ground coriander
- 15 g brown sugar
- 5 g coffee
- 5 g salt
- 2.5 g crushed fennel seeds
- 30 ml corn syrup
- 5 g dry yeast
- 45 g butter, melted

1. In a large bowl, mix the flour with coriander, sugar, coffee, salt, fennel seeds. Stir well to combine.
2. In a separate bowl, mix the warm water with cider vinegar, corn syrup, and melted butter. Stir until well combined and then leave it aside for 10 minutes.
3. Combine the two mixtures by adding the liquid mixture into the dry mixture. Stir until you obtain a dough, and then knead the dough.
4. Cover the dough and leave it aside for 2 hours to allow it to rise.
5. Shape the dough into 2 loaves, divide them into loaf pans, and leave them aside to rise for an additional 1 hour.

Rustic Rosemary Sourdough Bread

Prep time: 15 minutes | Cook time: 25 minutes | Serves 30

Rustic Rosemary Sourdough Bread is a delightful blend of the tangy sophistication of sourdough and the aromatic, earthy notes of fresh rosemary. Imagine a golden-brown loaf, its crust slightly crisp, and its crumb fragrant with the unmistakable scent of rosemary—a bread that not only satisfies your cravings but also transports you to the rustic charm of a Mediterranean kitchen.

At its core, this bread celebrates the magic of sourdough starter, which imparts a delightful tanginess and depth of flavor to the dough. The addition of rosemary leaves provides a burst of fragrance and a subtle herbaceous complexity. The result is a bread that's both rustic and refined, perfect for complementing a variety of dishes or simply enjoying on its own.

Savor Rustic Rosemary Sourdough Bread with a drizzle of olive oil, alongside a cheese platter, or as a companion to hearty soups and stews. Its rich aroma and herbaceous flavor make it an ideal addition to your table, whether you're dining al fresco or cozying up indoors.

Creating this bread is a culinary adventure that involves the art of sourdough fermentation and the careful infusion of rosemary. The sourdough starter is incorporated into the dough, allowing it to rise and develop its signature tangy flavor. Fresh rosemary leaves are gently folded into the mixture, ensuring even distribution and bursts of fragrance in every bite. Baking it to a golden perfection results in a loaf that captures the essence of Mediterranean cuisine and the simple joy of savoring a slice that's both rustic and aromatic.

Each bite of Rustic Rosemary Sourdough Bread is a reminder of the magic of combining classic sourdough with the fragrant elegance of rosemary—a true delight for those seeking a flavorful and aromatic bread option that embodies the beauty of Mediterranean flavors.

- 600g all-purpose unbleached flour
- 355g lukewarm water
- 227g ripe sourdough starter
- 5g instant yeast (use 10g if your sourdough isn't very vigorous)
- 15-20g chopped fresh rosemary
- 15g sea salt
- extra fresh rosemary and coarse salt (like fleur de sel) for sprinkling on the exterior

1. Combine all the ingredients in the bowl of a stand mixer fitted with the dough hook. Knead the mixture for 6-8 minutes on the "2" bread setting, or until a smooth dough forms. If you don't have a stand mixer, you can knead by hand, but it will take longer, approximately twice as long.
2. Shape the dough into a ball, spritz the bowl with oil, place the dough back in the bowl, and cover it loosely with plastic wrap. Allow the dough to rise in a warm area for about 90 minutes or until it has doubled in size.
3. After the first rise, punch down the dough to deflate it. Shape it into a round loaf, then place it in a banneton or a similar loaf pan, preferably one that is around 10 inches in diameter. Keep the dough covered and in a warm place for another hour or until it has nearly doubled in size. Preheat your oven to 425 degrees F (about 220 degrees C) during this time.

Almost No-Knead Fougasse

Prep time: 5 minutes | Cook time: 15 minutes | Makes 1 large fougasse

Almost No-Knead Fougasse is a delightful twist on the classic French bread, offering all the rustic charm with minimal effort. Imagine a beautifully shaped fougasse, its crust golden and crisp, and its crumb tender and airy—a bread that not only satisfies your cravings for French artisanal baking but also fits into your busy lifestyle.

At its core, this fougasse embraces the art of French breadmaking, with a simplified approach that requires less kneading. The result is a bread that's rustic, with its characteristic leaf or ear-like shape, and a delight to enjoy on its own or as a side to complement a wide range of dishes.

Almost No-Knead Fougasse is perfect for sharing at gatherings or as a special treat for yourself. Enjoy it dipped in olive oil and balsamic vinegar, or pair it with cheeses, charcuterie, or your favorite spreads. Its aroma and texture will transport you to the quaint bakeries of France, inviting you to savor the simple pleasures of homemade bread.

Creating this fougasse is a culinary adventure that involves minimal kneading and a longer fermentation period. The dough is allowed to rise and develop its characteristic texture and flavor. Shaping it into the traditional leaf pattern or any creative design you desire adds a touch of artistry to the process. Baking it to a golden perfection results in a fougasse that captures the essence of French baking and the joy of savoring a beautifully crafted bread.

Each bite of Almost No-Knead Fougasse is a reminder of the magic of French breadmaking and the satisfaction of enjoying a rustic bread that embodies the heart and soul of French cuisine. It's a bread that marries tradition with convenience, allowing you to experience the beauty of French baking with ease.

Dough:
- 50 g (¼ cup) bubbly, active starter
- 270 g (1 cup plus 2 tbsp) warm water
- 330 g (2¾ cups) bread flour
- 15 g (2 tbsp) whole wheat flour
- 5 g (1 tsp) fine sea salt
- cornmeal or semolina, for coating the pan

Toppings:
- olive oil, for brushing
- 2 g (2 tsp) herbes de provence
- parmesan cheese, to taste

Make the Dough:
1. Whisk the starter and water in a medium bowl with a fork. Add the flours and salt. Mix to combine, then finish by hand until a rough dough forms. Cover the bowl with a damp towel and let rest for 30 minutes. Replenish your starter with fresh flour and water, and store according to preference.
2. After the dough has rested, gently work the mass into a fairly smooth ball, about 15 seconds.

Bulk Rise:
1. Cover the bowl with a damp towel and let rise at room temperature until the dough has doubled in size. This will take about 8 to 10 hours, at 21°C.

Shape:
1. Line a sheet pan with parchment paper or a nonstick silicone mat. Sprinkle generously with cornmeal to prevent sticking. Remove the dough onto the sheet pan and let rest for 10 minutes. Gently flatten the dough into a 25-cm rectangle or oval shape, about 1.25 cm thick. Don't worry about being precise with your shaping—the dough should look rustic, not perfect.

Semolina Chili-Cheddar Loaf

Prep time: 10 minutes | Cook time: 40 minutes | Makes 1 loaf

The Semolina Chili-Cheddar Loaf is a delightful fusion of spicy chili heat and the creamy richness of cheddar cheese, all wrapped up in a golden loaf. Imagine slices of this bread, each one boasting a tender crumb studded with spicy chili flakes and pockets of melted cheddar—a bread that not only satisfies your cravings but also adds a bold twist with its exciting flavors.

At its core, this loaf celebrates the versatility of semolina flour, known for its slightly gritty texture and distinct flavor. The addition of spicy chili flakes and sharp cheddar cheese creates a bread that's both hearty and thrilling, perfect for sandwiches, toast, or as a unique addition to your cheese platter.

Savor the Semolina Chili-Cheddar Loaf toasted with a smear of butter or paired with your favorite dips. Its aroma and flavor will transport you to a world of bold and savory delights, inviting you to savor the simple pleasures of homemade bread with a kick.

Creating this loaf is a culinary adventure that involves the art of breadmaking and the careful balance of ingredients. Baking it to a golden brown results in a loaf that captures the essence of bold flavors and the simple joy of savoring a slice packed with excitement.

Each bite of the Semolina Chili-Cheddar Loaf is a reminder of the magic of combining unexpected spicy. It's a bread that embraces the thrill of flavor experimentation while celebrating the comforting allure of homemade goodness—a true delight for those seeking an adventure in every bite.

- 280 g (2⅓ cups) bread flour
- 80 g (⅔ cup) fine semolina flour
- 282 g (1¼ cups) warm water
- 75 g (⅓ cup) active sourdough starter
- 7 g (1 tsp) salt
- 58 g (½ cup) thinly sliced cheddar cheese
- 22 g (¼ cup) sliced Fresno chilies

Day 1:

1. In a large mixing bowl, combine the bread flour, semolina flour and water. Mix until all the flour is hydrated. Cover the bowl with plastic wrap and allow dough to autolyze for 1 hour.
2. In another large mixing bowl, combine the autolyzed dough, active starter and salt. Keep folding until the mixture forms a cohesive, homogenous dough. Cover the bowl with plastic wrap and set aside for 30 minutes.
3. Wet your countertop slightly, turn your dough out and flatten it into a rectangle. Spread the cheese and peppers evenly over the top. Use your hands to roll the dough into a log, flatten it slightly and fold the ends toward the middle. Return the stuffed dough to the bowl. Cover with plastic wrap and set aside for 30 minutes.

Day 2:

1. Put your Dutch oven in the oven and preheat it to 260°C. Score your loaf and gently place it in the hot Dutch oven. Bake covered for 30 minutes and uncovered for 10 to 15 minutes.
2. Place the loaf on a wire rack and allow it to cool for at least 2 hours before slicing. Store leftover bread in a paper bag in more humid climates or in a plastic bag in drier environments.

Roasted Garlic Sourdough Bread

Prep time: 9 hours | Cook time: 9 hours 40 minutes |
Makes 1 loaf

Roasted Garlic Sourdough Bread is a delightful blend of the tangy sophistication of sourdough and the savory allure of roasted garlic. Imagine a golden-brown loaf, its crust slightly crisp, and its crumb infused with the rich, earthy aroma and flavor of roasted garlic—a bread that not only satisfies your cravings but also elevates your palate with a symphony of flavors.

At its core, this bread celebrates the magic of sourdough starter, which imparts a delightful tanginess and depth of flavor to the dough. The addition of roasted garlic cloves provides a savory complexity and an aromatic richness. The result is a bread that's both rustic and refined, perfect for enjoying as a side or creating gourmet sandwiches.

Savor Roasted Garlic Sourdough Bread with a drizzle of olive oil, as the perfect accompaniment to roasted vegetables, or paired with your favorite cheeses. Its rich aroma and savory notes make it an ideal addition to your table, whether you're hosting a gathering or indulging in a quiet meal.

Creating this bread is a culinary adventure that involves the art of sourdough fermentation and the careful roasting of garlic. Baking it to a golden perfection results in a loaf that captures the essence of gourmet breadmaking and the simple joy of savoring a slice that's both flavorful and aromatic.

Each bite of Roasted Garlic Sourdough Bread is a reminder of the magic of combining classic sourdough with the savory depth of roasted garlic—a true delight for those seeking a bread that's both sophisticated and comforting, with a savory twist that elevates the experience of homemade goodness.

Tools Needed:
6-quart Dutch oven, bread lame or very sharp knife, spray bottle

For Activating the Starter:

- 135 grams (1/2 cup) sourdough starter
- 120 milliliters (1/2 cup) lukewarm (32°C to 38°C) pure filtered or bottled water
- 115 grams (1 cup) whole-wheat flour

For the Bread Dough:

- 68 grams (1/4 cup) active sourdough starter
- 360 milliliters (1 1/2 cups) warm (38°C to 52°C) pure filtered or bottled water
- 454 grams (just under 4 cups) unbleached bread flour, plus more for dusting
- 57 grams (1/2 cup) whole-wheat flour
- 1 1/2 teaspoons fine sea salt
- 1 head garlic, roasted

To Activate the Starter:
1. At least 6 to 12 hours prior to making the dough, in a medium bowl, combine the starter, lukewarm water, and flour, completely incorporating the ingredients into the starter. Loosely cover and let sit on the counter until ready to use.

To Make the Bread Dough:
1. In a large bowl, stir together the active starter, warm water, bread flour, and whole-wheat flour, mixing until combined. Cover the bowl with a clean kitchen towel and let rest for 30 minutes.
2. Add the salt and, in the bowl, knead it in by folding the dough over and pushing on it. Continue kneading until the dough forms a smooth ball and begins to tighten. Spread the dough out a bit, add the roasted garlic cloves, and knead them in, trying to evenly distribute them without crushing.
3. Cover the dough with a clean damp kitchen towel and let rest at room temperature (about 24°C) until doubled in size, about 8 hours.
4. Lightly flour a breadboard or clean work surface and turn the dough out onto it. Using floured hands, shape the dough into a circle by continually tucking the edges under as you turn the ball.
5. Place the dough seam-side up into a well-floured banneton basket or into a small bowl lined with a well-floured kitchen towel. Cover the dough with another floured kitchen towel. Let rise for 30 minutes to 1 hour.
6. Preheat the oven to 230°C. Place a Dutch oven, with its lid on, in the oven.
7. of minutes before transferring it to a wire rack to cool completely before slicing.

Rustic Honey and Oat Loaf

Prep time: 10 minutes | Cook time: 1 hour| Serves 4

The Rustic Honey and Oat Loaf is a delightful blend of sweet honey and the hearty goodness of oats, resulting in a bread that's both comforting and flavorful. Imagine slices of this golden-brown loaf, each one boasting a tender crumb enriched with the natural sweetness of honey and the delightful crunch of oats—a bread that not only satisfies your cravings but also brings a sweet, rustic charm to your table.

At its core, this loaf celebrates the beauty of simple, wholesome ingredients. Honey adds a touch of sweetness and moisture, while oats provide a satisfying texture and nutty flavor. The result is a bread that's perfect for breakfast, toasted with butter, or as a complement to a variety of dishes.

Savor the Rustic Honey and Oat Loaf with a drizzle of honey or a spread of your favorite fruit preserves. Its warm aroma and delightful crunch make it an ideal addition to your morning routine, or as a companion to your cheese and charcuterie platters.

Creating this loaf is a culinary adventure that involves the art of breadmaking and the careful blending of honey and oats. The dough is prepared with care, allowing it to rise and develop its characteristic texture and flavor. Baking it to a golden brown results in a loaf that captures the essence of rustic bread and the simple joy of savoring a slice packed with natural sweetness and wholesome goodness.

Each bite of the Rustic Honey and Oat Loaf is a reminder of the magic of combining timeless ingredients to create a bread that's both comforting and flavorful. It's a bread that embodies the warmth of honey and the satisfying crunch of oats—a true delight for those seeking a taste of rustic charm in their homemade bread.

Levain:
- 30 g active starter
- 60 g warm water
- 30 g buckwheat flour
- 30 g brown rice flour

Loaf:
- 20 g whole gluten-free oats
- 60 g cold milk
- 70 g sorghum flour
- 65 g tapioca starch
- 30 g millet flour
- 30 g buckwheat flour
- 30 g brown rice flour
- 9 g salt
- 280 g warm water
- 50 g honey
- 12 g molasses
- 23 g whole psyllium husk
- White rice flour, as needed

Topping:
- 30 g whole gluten-free oats

1. Reactivate your starter the day before you plan on building the levain. A good time to do this is when you get up in the morning, to allow the starter 6 to 8 hours to become bubbly and active. You will need 30 grams for the levain and at least 20 grams for maintaining your original starter/ main culture.
2. Build the levain: Weigh 30 grams of active starter in a clean 500-milliliter jar, then add 60 grams of warm water and vigorously whisk the ingredients together. Add the 30 grams of buckwheat flour and the 30 grams of brown rice flour. Ferment the levain for 6 to 8 hours, or until it is bubbling and it has risen to a peak, before mixing it into the dough.
3. Mix the dough: In a medium saucepan, combine the oats and cold milk. Cook the oats over medium-low heat for 3 to 4 minutes, stirring them occasionally, until they have absorbed all the milk. Set the oats aside to cool for about 10 minutes, or until they are not hot to the touch. In a large bowl, combine the sorghum flour, tapioca starch, millet flour, buckwheat flour, brown rice flour and salt. Mix the dough well by hand, or with a kitchen mixer fitted with a dough hook running at medium-low speed, until all the ingredients are fully incorporated.
4. Ferment: Form the dough into a ball, then place it in a 4-cup (1-L) proofing bowl. Cover the bowl with its lid and place the bowl in the oven with the light on. Let the dough rest for 30 to 60 minutes, or until the dough begins to rise a little. Place the covered bowl in the fridge overnight for the bulk fermentation.
5. Shape: the next day, remove the dough from the fridge and leave it at room temperature for about 30 minutes, until it is warm enough to work with. Liberally dust a 18-cm banneton with the white rice flour. Sprinkle a little of the white rice flour on the dough's surface, then repeat the kneading process for about 1 minute. With cupped hands, drag the dough in small circles to shape it into a smooth ball. Pinch, seal and smooth any seams in the dough. Scoop the dough up with a bench scraper and gently place it seam side up in the prepared banneton.

Cranberry and Hazelnut Bread

Prep time: 10 minutes | Cook time: 55 minutes| Serves 4

Loaf:
- 80 g dried cranberries
- 100 g fresh orange juice, at room temperature
- 50 g sorghum flour
- 40 g buckwheat flour
- 60 g oat flour
- 65 g tapioca starch
- 50 g white rice flour, plus more as needed
- 40 g hazelnuts, roughly chopped
- 8 g salt
- 200 g warm water
- 10 g molasses
- 20 g honey
- 18 g whole psyllium husk
- 5 g flaxseed, finely ground

Cranberry and Hazelnut Bread is a delightful blend of tart cranberries and the earthy richness of hazelnuts, resulting in a bread that's both satisfying and bursting with flavor. Imagine slices of this golden-brown loaf, each one featuring a tender crumb punctuated by the tartness of cranberries and the delightful crunch of toasted hazelnuts—a bread that not only satisfies your cravings but also adds a touch of gourmet sophistication to your table.

At its core, this bread celebrates the beauty of combining vibrant, natural ingredients. The cranberries bring a burst of tartness and color, while the hazelnuts provide a satisfying nuttiness and crunch. The result is a bread that's perfect for breakfast, brunch, or as a complement to a variety of dishes.

Savor Cranberry and Hazelnut Bread with a smear of butter, a drizzle of honey, or paired with soft cheeses. Its rich aroma and delightful textures make it an ideal addition to your table, whether you're hosting a festive gathering or enjoying a cozy meal at home.

Creating this bread is a culinary adventure that involves the art of breadmaking and the careful combination of cranberries and hazelnuts. The dough is prepared with care, allowing it to rise and develop its characteristic texture and flavor. Baking it to a golden perfection results in a loaf that captures the essence of gourmet bread and the simple joy of savoring a slice filled with vibrant tartness and nutty goodness.

Each bite of Cranberry and Hazelnut Bread is a reminder of the magic of combining diverse ingredients to create a bread that's both elegant and comforting. It's a bread that embodies the contrast of tart cranberries and toasted hazelnuts—a true delight for those seeking a flavorful and textural adventure in their homemade bread.

Levain:
- 60 g active starter
- 120 g warm water
- 60 g buckwheat flour
- 60 g brown rice flour

1. Reactivate your starter the day before you plan on building the levain. A good time to do this is when you get up in the morning, to allow the starter 6 to 8 hours to become bubbly and active. You will need 60 grams for the levain and at least 20 grams left over for maintaining your original starter/main culture.

2. Build the levain: Using a kitchen scale, weigh 60 grams of active starter in a clean 500-milliliter jar. Add 120 grams of warm water and vigorously whisk the starter and water together. Add 60 grams of buckwheat flour and 60 grams of brown rice flour. Ferment the levain for 6 to 8 hours, or until it is bubbly and has risen to a peak, before mixing it into the dough.

3. Mix the dough: In a small bowl, soak the cranberries in the orange juice for up to 2 hours or overnight in the fridge to plump them up. Immediately whisk the psyllium gel to prevent lumps from forming, then whisk in the levain and cranberries (no need to drain the cranberries, as they should absorb most of the juice). Add this mixture to the flour blend. Mix the dough well by hand, or with a kitchen mixer fitted with a dough hook running at medium-low speed, until all the ingredients are fully incorporated.

4. Ferment: Form the dough into a ball, then place it in a 4-cup proofing bowl. Cover the bowl with its lid and place it in the oven with the light on. Let the dough rest for 30 to 60 minutes, or until the dough begins to rise a little. Place the covered bowl in the fridge overnight for the bulk fermentation.

5. Shape: the next day, remove the dough from the fridge and leave it at room temperature for about 30 minutes, until it is warm enough to work with. Liberally dust a 18-cm banneton with the additional white rice flour. Lightly dampen a work surface with water. With cupped hands, drag the dough in small circles to shape it into a smooth ball. Poke any exposed cranberries back inside the dough and knead it a little more to smooth its surface. Shape the dough into a ball and gently place the dough seam side up in the prepared banneton.

Appendix 1 Measurement Conversion Chart

Volume Equivalents (Dry)

US STANDARD	METRIC (APPROXIMATE)
1/8 teaspoon	0.5 mL
1/4 teaspoon	1 mL
1/2 teaspoon	2 mL
3/4 teaspoon	4 mL
1 teaspoon	5 mL
1 tablespoon	15 mL
1/4 cup	59 mL
1/2 cup	118 mL
3/4 cup	177 mL
1 cup	235 mL
2 cups	475 mL
3 cups	700 mL
4 cups	1 L

Volume Equivalents (Liquid)

US STANDARD	US STANDARD (OUNCES)	METRIC (APPROXIMATE)
2 tablespoons	1 fl.oz.	30 mL
1/4 cup	2 fl.oz.	60 mL
1/2 cup	4 fl.oz.	120 mL
1 cup	8 fl.oz.	240 mL
1 1/2 cup	12 fl.oz.	355 mL
2 cups or 1 pint	16 fl.oz.	475 mL
4 cups or 1 quart	32 fl.oz.	1 L
1 gallon	128 fl.oz.	4 L

Temperatures Equivalents

FAHRENHEIT(F)	CELSIUS(C) APPROXIMATE
225 °F	107 °C
250 °F	120 ° °C
275 °F	135 °C
300 °F	150 °C
325 °F	160 °C
350 °F	180 °C
375 °F	190 °C
400 °F	205 °C
425 °F	220 °C
450 °F	235 °C
475 °F	245 °C
500 °F	260 °C

Weight Equivalents

US STANDARD	METRIC (APPROXIMATE)
1 ounce	28 g
2 ounces	57 g
5 ounces	142 g
10 ounces	284 g
15 ounces	425 g
16 ounces (1 pound)	455 g
1.5 pounds	680 g
2 pounds	907 g

Appendix 2 The Dirty Dozen and Clean Fifteen

The Environmental Working Group (EWG) is a nonprofit, nonpartisan organization dedicated to protecting human health and the environment Its mission is to empower people to live healthier lives in a healthier environment. This organization publishes an annual list of the twelve kinds of produce, in sequence, that have the highest amount of pesticide residue-the Dirty Dozen-as well as a list of the fifteen kinds ofproduce that have the least amount of pesticide residue-the Clean Fifteen.

THE DIRTY DOZEN	
The 2016 Dirty Dozen includes the following produce. These are considered among the year's most important produce to buy organic:	
Strawberries	Spinach
Apples	Tomatoes
Nectarines	Bell peppers
Peaches	Cherry tomatoes
Celery	Cucumbers
Grapes	Kale/collard greens
Cherries	Hot peppers

The Dirty Dozen list contains two additional itemskale/collard greens and hot peppers-because they tend to contain trace levels of highly hazardous pesticides.

THE CLEAN FIFTEEN	
The least critical to buy organically are the Clean Fifteen list. The following are on the 2016 list:	
Avocados	Papayas
Corn	Kiw
Pineapples	Eggplant
Cabbage	Honeydew
Sweet peas	Grapefruit
Onions	Cantaloupe
Asparagus	Cauliflower
Mangos	

Some of the sweet corn sold in the United States are made from genetically engineered (GE) seedstock. Buy organic varieties of these crops to avoid GE produce.

Appendix 3 Index

Gloria J. Williams